MW00616295

PRESENTED TO:

____

FROM:

____

DATE:

____

INSIDE OUT

A 40 DAY JOURNEY TO TRANSFORMING YOUR HEART

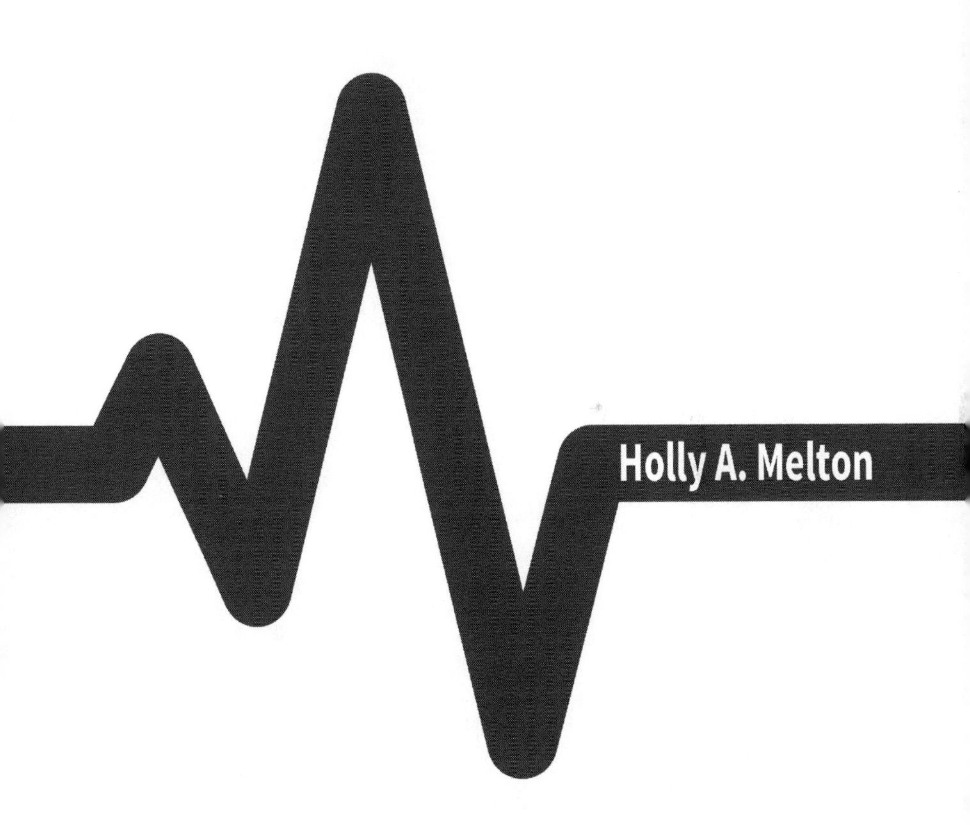

Additional Copies
https://www.amazon.com
https://www.mattandhollymelton.org/store

TABLE OF CONTENTS

DAY 1
HEART ATTACK!

"HEART ATTACK! I think I'm having a HEART ATTACK!" These are not the words you want to hear coming from your mouth. Unexpected heart attacks occur because we can't physically see our hearts' health and aren't intentional in keeping it healthy.

Our hearts are the most critical organ in our body. From it flows the blood that brings us life. When our heart stops working correctly, we stop working correctly. Often, we don't think about strengthening our physical heart because we can't see it. It's out of sight, out of mind. Exercise is good for the heart. But that takes time, commitment and endurance. Oxygen is good for the heart. But sometimes, with the anxiety and stresses of life, it's hard to breathe. Peace is good for the heart, but sometimes fear and uncertainty overwhelm us, and our heart beats faster than it should. When we don't regularly consider keeping our hearts healthy, we become susceptible to a life-threatening heart attack.

It is the same with our spiritual hearts. We do not know how unhealthy, how sick our hearts are until, all of a sudden, we find ourselves giving in to some sort of sin that we'd never thought we would do. HEART ATTACK. Or we say something that destroys a relationship, and we can't believe those words came out of our mouths. HEART ATTACK. We cannot prevent these attacks on our own because we don't even realize where we are spiritually sick.

How can we protect ourselves from a spiritual heart attack?

Proverbs 4:23 says,

> "Keep your heart with all vigilance, for from it flow the springs of life."

We need to learn the depth of our hearts. We cannot see things on our own, but God can reveal them to us when we ask Him. If we take time to focus on our physical hearts health by changing our eating habits, exercising, and monitoring our hearts, our health will change! That is true with our spiritual hearts. When we take time to focus on what's inside and are open to purging out what is killing us, we will live the abundant life that Jesus promised us.

This 40-day journey will be like open-heart surgery on our spiritual hearts. Maybe you don't feel you need surgery. Your heart isn't that bad!

The Bible says differently in Jeremiah 17:9,

> "The heart is deceitful above all things, and desperately sick; who can understand it?"

If we don't realize the depth of the depravity, the deception, and the desires of the flesh growing in our hearts daily, we will become very spiritually sick. You may say, "But…but…surgery is scary!" Yes, but it is necessary to help our hearts function properly and thrive in life. Surgery requires desperation. This is the only way to get the help we need. It requires complete surrender to the Great Surgeon and Healer, God. Only He can make our hearts clean and new.

This journey may be humbling, but, I pray, it also fills you with hope. We do not have to have our hearts under attack. We can attack the unhealthy places inside us with vigilance and come out victorious. Let's start looking from the Inside Out and live the life God's planned for us!

> "As in water face reflects face, so the heart of man reflects the man." -Proverbs 27:19

> "The purpose in a man's heart is like deep water, but a man of understanding will draw it out." -Proverbs 20:5

TAKE A MOMENT

1. Where have you experienced a spiritual "heart attack" in the past? How did it affect you and others?

2. Why are you resolving to commit to this journey toward your spiritual health? How will it benefit you and others to be vigilant with your heart's health?

> *Heavenly Father, you are my Creator. You are my Surgeon. You are my Healer. I come to You longing to have my heart become healthy. Show me where my heart is deceiving me and making me sick. May Your Spirit open my eyes to the areas I need to work on and help me to work on them with all vigilance. I begin this journey with great expectancy that You will bring victory in my life from the inside out! Amen.*

DAY 2
LET THE EXAM BEGIN!

Examinations. This word can bring a bit of anxiety. Whether a doctor examines us to find out our health status or we take an examination to find out the depth of our knowledge on a subject, exams expose us to a reality we may not want to embrace.

Psalm 139:1 says,

> "O Lord, you have examined my heart and know everything about me." *(NLT)*

Hmmm..let's take that in for a moment. God examines our hearts. "Examine" means to investigate something thorougly to determine its condition. God is thoroughly investigating us. He is the original Sherlock Holmes. He is consistently evaluating how we are doing. He knows everything about us at every moment. He knows our desires and dreams. He knows our worst nightmares and greatest fears. He knows the trauma we've experienced. He knows the abuse we've endured. He knows our highest joys and our deepest sorrows. He knows the steps of faith we've taken. He knows where we've failed. He knows our personality and spiritual gifts. He knows what we value in life and why. He knows our secret sins. He knows where we feel shame, doubt, and discouragement. He knows us better than we know ourselves. Why? Because He created us. He created you.

Interestingly enough, God still examines our hearts as if He didn't know everything about us. Why is that? In God's perfect design, He did not plan for us to be born sinners. The first man and woman that God created chose to make their own decisions apart from what God commanded, and ever since then, every person who is born has a heart that is blemished with sin. It's hard to imagine a newborn baby and not see pure innocence. But wait a week, or a month, and you will see that even the heart of a newborn is full of selfishness, anger and a demanding spirit. They have no clue how their selfishness is challenging their parents' patience. Just as a baby is unaware of their sin, we are often unaware of our sin and how it affects us and those around us.

God's examination of our heart is not to condemn us. He examines us so that He can bring hope and healing to the most broken parts of our lives. He does this by offering His presence, His protection, and His peace. We will never experience what He is freely offering if we don't acknowledge our hearts' current status. When we ignore His examination results, we aren't giving Him access to those places that need healing and hope. That means peace will elude us.

What is the use if we go to a doctor, have an exam, receive the report, and do nothing about it? The exam exposes what is going on inside of us so that the work toward healing can begin. To heal our spiritual hearts, we must begin by inviting God to search our hearts and tell us what He finds.

Psalm 139:23 says,

> "Search me, O God, and know my heart! Try me and know my thoughts!"

We are not asking this because He is unaware of what is inside us. We are asking this because we are unaware of what is inside of us. When we ask God to reveal to us what He's discovered in His search, then we can join Him in the journey to transform our hearts from the inside out!

> "And you, Solomon my son, know the God of your father and serve him with a whole heart and with a willing mind, for the LORD searches all hearts and understands every plan and thought. If you seek him, he will be found by you, but if you forsake him, he will cast you off forever." -1 Chronicles 28:9

> "I the Lord search the heart and test the mind, to give every man according to his ways, according to the fruit of his deeds." -Jeremiah 17:10

TAKE A MOMENT

1. What are your fears in allowing God to reveal to you your heart?
2. How can you choose to trust that this examination is for your good?

> *Heavenly Father, You know me because You created me. You examine my heart because You love me and want me to know what is going on inside me so that together we can be on a journey of healing. I choose by faith to trust that what You reveal to me about my heart is not to condemn me but to work Your plan of sanctification in my life. You want me to become more like You from the inside out. Please reveal to me my heart so that I can change and heal. Amen.*

DAY 3
MIND READER

Have you ever thought about what it'd be like to have the sixth sense to read people's minds? How would it affect our view of others if we could know what they thought about us or other things in life? Would we grow to admire them more, or would we grow in disgust with what we uncover? What if someone could do that with you? If someone could know your every thought, would you feel understood, or would you feel exposed?

God is the ultimate mind reader. He knows our every thought.

It says in Psalm 139:2,

> "You know when I sit down and when I rise up; you discern my thoughts from afar."

He knows what our minds mull over, spin-on, and what makes us lose sleep because we just can't seem to shut our brains off. Our thoughts consume us, overwhelm us, condemn us, and we become sleepless, joyless zombies that just try to get through one more day. How can we make it stop?

Our thoughts come from our hearts. And as we've already discussed, our hearts deceive us. We cannot trust what we think is true or right.

Proverbs 28:26 says,

> "Whoever trusts in his own mind is a fool, but he who walks in wisdom will be delivered."

Jesus teaches that what defiles us begins in our thoughts.

Mark 7:20-22 says,

> "What comes out of a person is what defiles him. For from within, out of the heart of man, comes evil thoughts, sexual immorality, theft, murder, adultery, coveting, wickedness, deceit, sensuality, envy, slander, pride, foolishness. All these evil things come from within, and they defile a person."

When we think about something and allow ourselves to meditate on it, it is then that the thought can turn to action. One small action can lead to a slightly bigger action until we notice our thoughts not only have led us astray, they now control us. For example, we may see a beautiful man or woman and have impure thoughts. That meditation may lead to looking at enticing pictures or videos that then lead to inappropriate behaviors. These behaviors can lead to sexual addictions and destroy our ability to have healthy, intimate relationships with others.

If we want to change our actions, we must begin by changing our thoughts. To change our thoughts, we must immerse ourselves in the truth only found in the Word of God. It is there that our minds will focus on God and how to think rightly to become more like Him.

Romans 12:2 says,

> "Do not be conformed to this world, but be transformed by the renewal of your mind, that by testing you may discern what is the will of God, what is good and acceptable and perfect."

When we fill our minds with the Word of God, our thoughts align with how God sees us and how God sees others. We can begin by studying the promises of God and what the Bible says about our thought life. When we do this, we will not look lustfully at others because they are created in God's image and should be respected. We will not slander others because we do not want to shame them. We will not covet because we are thankful for the spiritual inheritance we have in Christ. We will not envy because we see that God gives us specific gifts and abilities to use for His glory. We will not be prideful because we know our great need for Jesus to forgive us for our sins daily.

Philippians 4:8 helps us to evaluate what we are to think about,

> "Finally brothers, whatever is true, whatever is honoable, whatever is just, whatever is pure, whatever is lovely, whatever is commendable, if there is any excellence, if there is anything worthy of praise, think about these things."

God knows our thoughts. He is the ultimate mind reader. He provides us with His Word to refocus our thoughts on what is good, acceptable, and perfect. We will be transformed from the inside out when we are intentional to renew our thoughts, one at a time, with His Word.

> "The Lord saw that the wickedness of man was great in the earth, and that every intention of the thoughts of his heart was only evil continually." -Genesis 6:5

> "But Jesus, knowing their thoughts, said, 'Why do you think evil in your hearts?'" -Matthew 9:4

> "O Jerusalem, wash your heart from evil, that you may be saved. How long shall your wicked thoughts lodge within you?" -Jeremiah 4:14

> "For the word of God is living and active, sharper than any two-edged sword, piercing to the division of soul and of spirit, of joints and of marrow, and discerning the thoughts and intentions of the heart." -Hebrews 4:12

TAKE A MOMENT

1. What thoughts consume you?

2. How can faithfully immersing yourself in the Word of God help you with your thoughts? How can this change your actions?

> *Heavenly Father, thank You that You do not want me to be a slave to my thoughts. Thank You that You have given me Your Word to help transform my mind. Help me to go to You when I know my thoughts are impure. Thank You that You know my thoughts and still give me grace and mercy so that I can fight this battle over my mind. In the name of Jesus, I surrender my thoughts on ___________ to You. Renew my mind with Your Word. Take back control of my mind so that I can honor You with my thoughts and transform from the inside out. Amen.*

DAY 4
SECRETS

Secrets. We've all had them. A secret is something we keep private. It is something we want to remain unknown or unseen by others. Often it is something about ourselves. Something we've said. Something we've done. Something that's been done to us.

If we are brave enough to share our secrets with someone, we often ask that they not tell anyone else. If they do, we feel exposed, and trust is broken. It is rare to find someone we can trust with our secrets. We fear they will condemn us, or they might share our most humiliating, embarrassing moments with others.

Secrets began when sin entered the world. The first man and woman chose to make their own decisions with their own wisdom and decided not to obey God's commands. He told them not to eat the fruit from one specific tree. Only one thing was forbidden. Yet, they couldn't withhold themselves from trying it. As soon as they tasted it, they knew they had sinned and immediately hid from God. They did not want Him to know what they had done. But He did know, didn't He? We can't hide from God. He sees what we choose to do. He sees where we choose to go. He hears what we choose to say.

Psalm 44:20-21 says,

> "If we had forgotten the name of our God or spread out our hands to a foreign god, would not God discover this? For he knows the secrets of the heart."

God knows our secrets. But He also sees what's inside us. He knows how we are feeling about what we did or said. He knows when we have walked away from Him and embraced something that is forbidden. God also knows how it's tearing us up inside.

We aren't meant to keep secrets hidden. When held deep inside, secrets isolate us, condemn us, and eventually destroy us. It seems funny now, but in middle school, I told my friends that I had leukemia. I lied to them because I thought if they believed I was sick, they'd have compassion for me and be my friend. This secret lie consumed me. My solution was to tell my friends I was in remission and no longer had cancer. Unfortunately, the new lie that covered up the old one didn't free me. I felt so convicted, but I couldn't admit it was all a lie. I got to the point where I asked God to give me cancer because I believed that having it, no matter the struggle or possible results, would be better than the pain of living a lie. The Lord faithfully convicted me for over six years, and finally, at the end of my senior year, I confessed to a group of friends that I never had cancer. Surprisingly, they embraced me, and with their forgiveness, I felt free. Only when I bravely shared my secret could I move forward in freedom, joy, hope, and experience God's blessings in my life.

God knows you want to be set free from the burden of holding onto secrets. He knows that you long to be right with Him and others. He sees your heart. Listen to what God said to the Prophet Samuel when he was examining Eliab, one of David's older brothers, as the potential next King of Israel,

> "Do not look on his appearance or on the height of his stature, because I have rejected him. For the Lord sees not as man see: man looks on the outward appearance, but the Lord looks on the heart" -1 Samuel 16:7

God chose David to be king because of his heart. He was humble. David was known as a man after God's own heart *(Acts 13:22)*. Yet, David didn't live a sinless life. After becoming king, he secretly committed adultery and then murder, so that, he could have another man's wife. Those are huge secrets. How did he recover from that? He humbled himself by confessing his secret sins to God, and God forgave him. God didn't just forgive him; God blessed him. It would be through his lineage that our ultimate King, Jesus, would be born.

God doesn't care who you appear to be on the outside. He isn't impressed with your achievements, titles, or goals. He cares about your heart. When you get your heart right with God by humbly confessing your secret *(that He already knows)*, you will be able to experience freedom, joy, hope, and His blessings in your life. Exposing what's inside is scary. But when you expose yourself to God, He will graciously come alongside you, forgive you, and begin to rebuild your life from the inside out.

> "And to the angel of the church in Thyatira write: 'The words of the Son of God, who has eyes like a flame of fire, and whose feet are like burnished bronze. "'I know your works, your love and faith and service and patient endurance, and that your latter works exceed the first. But I have this against you, that you tolerate that woman Jezebel, who calls herself a prophetess and is teaching and seducing my servants to practice sexual immorality and to eat food sacrificed to idols. I gave her time to repent, but she refuses to repent of her sexual immorality. Behold, I will throw her onto a sickbed, and those who commit adultery with her I will throw into great tribulation, unless they repent of her works, And I will strike her children dead. And all the churches will know that I am he who searches mind and heart, and I will give to each of you according to your works."
> -Revelation 2:18-23

TAKE A MOMENT

1. What secrets have you been holding onto that you need to share with God and others openly?

2. What are the benefits to risk and share with Him what He already knows? What are the possible consequences if you don't?

> *Heavenly Father, there are no secrets between You and me. You know everything. It is hard to be vulnerable and admit my secrets because shame is involved. But You took my sin and my shame and put it on the cross when Jesus died for me. Thank You that I can admit anything to You, and You will come alongside me, forgive me, and reestablish an honest, trusting relationship with You. I know I cannot be transformed from the inside out unless I confess my secrets to You. So, here is what I want to confess today _______________. Thank You for knowing my heart and forgiving me. I ask that You will now rebuild my life and use my life for Your glory. Amen.*

DAY 5
UNDER FIRE

"Under fire" literally means to be attacked with guns or with severe criticism. Those who have fought in combat best understand what it is like to be under fire. They have a heightened awareness that an attack can happen at any moment. They are trained soldiers, yet they cannot plan with certainty what may happen next. They move cautiously and with courage. They risk their lives so that we can experience freedom.

Many followers of Jesus worldwide understand what "under fire" means also. They are unashamed of the gospel in places where the gospel is criticized and where their faith may lead to death. They, too, move cautiously and with courage. They also risk their lives so that their people might hear the gospel and experience freedom.

I experienced being "under fire" when I visited a missionary team in the Middle East. This country is 100% Muslim. We couldn't find a single secret church of believers. Even as foreigners, we had to wear an abaya, a long, black covering, like a graduation gown. We wore a niqab, a veil, to cover our hair. Since we were not Muslim, we were required to wear colorful veils, not the traditional black niqabs worn by women.

One evening, as we were on the busy streets in the capital city, a jeep full of military men with machine guns started to pass us slowly. Their foul language and criticism were intimidating, but it was when they shot their machine guns off into the sky that our knees buckled and we collapsed to the ground. They were making a point. Foreigners are not welcome. Our faith is not welcome. One of the missionaries said to me, "Every day, we wonder if we will make it out of the country alive. We choose to stay, praying that our presence here will lead at least one person to faith in Jesus."

My friends bravely lived out 1 Thessalonians 2:4, which says,

> "But just as we have been approved by God to be entrusted with the gospel, so we speak, not to please man, but to please God who tests our hearts."

Proverbs 17:3 says,

> "The crucible is for silver, and the furnace is for gold, and the Lord tests hearts."

God allows our faith to go "under fire" to see if it is real. We may not have to fear a gun pointing at us for our faith in the United States, but we may fear criticism. Having a Biblical world view is no longer popular in America. It is seen as antiquated and archaic. Our faith is under fire, and we must decide if we will stand as soldiers for Christ and be unashamed of the gospel, or if we will shrink back, fear what people think of us, and become useless in bringing others the hope and freedom of the gospel.

God has approved us to be His soldiers. God is entrusting us with the eternal gift of the gospel. The question is, do our hearts care to share it with others? Do we grasp what freedom we have through Christ in such a way that we want to bless others with the same freedom? Sharing the gospel is a risk, but so is fighting in a war. What better battle to be a part of than for others' souls? God wants to see if we are ashamed of the gospel or if we grasp that it is the most fantastic news we could share with our family, friends, neighbors, and co-workers.

Sharing the gospel may be intimidating at first. We may not know how to bring up spiritual things. Thank goodness, God does. He knows what people need to hear to consider Jesus. When we invite God into our conversations with others, He will guide us on what to say. He's just waiting for us to be courageous and enlist as His ambassadors.

When we take steps of faith to be unashamed of the gospel, something new is created within our hearts. We gain a deeper heart for the lost. We have eyes to see the lives around us and how to enter in to care for them and bring them the hope of the gospel. When we see a person experience freedom from receiving the grace of the gospel, we can't go back. Our hearts will no longer fear man but will please God by publicly living out and sharing our faith. Will we be courageous even when our faith is under fire and share the gospel? We can't transform from the inside out until we allow God to test our hearts and begin to be unashamed of the gospel.

> "Oh, let the evil of the wicked come to an end, and may you establish the righteous-you who test the minds and hearts, O righteous God!" -Psalm 7:9

> "Prove me, O Lord, and try me; test my heart and my mind." -Psalm 26:2

> "Yet if anyone suffers as a Christian, let him not be ashamed, but let him glorify God in that name." -1 Peter 4:15

> "For this reason I remind you to fan into flame the gift of God, which is in you through the laying on of my hands, for God gave us a spirit not of fear but of power and love and self-control. Therefore do not be ashamed of the testimony about our Lord, nor of me his prisoner, but share in suffering for the gospel by the power of God, who saved us and called us to a holy calling, not because of our works but because of his own purpose and grace, which he gave us in Christ Jesus before the ages began." -2 Timothy 1:6-9

TAKE A MOMENT

1. What fears do you have in living out your faith publicly?
2. Why is it worth the risk and criticism to do so?

> *Heavenly Father, thank You for the amazing gift of the gospel. I know You want me to share it with others, even if I feel under fire and am criticized for my faith. Please give me the heart to care for the lost people around me. Give me the courage to step out in faith to talk to them. Give me the wisdom to know what to say. I want to be Your ambassador and be unashamed of the gospel. Help me to keep my eyes on You. Amen.*

DAY 6

AFRAID OF THE LIGHT

Children seem to learn to be afraid of the dark at quite a young age. Whether it's the boogie man, monsters under the bed, or fearing bad guys will come to get them after watching the Christmas movie, "Home Alone," children know that darkness feels unsafe.

On the other hand, adults seem to be afraid of the light. We'd rather live in denial than look at the darkness in our hearts and admit that we need God to shine His pure, holy, convicting light into all areas of our lives. Plato wisely said, "We can easily forgive a child who is afraid of the dark; the real tragedy of life is when men are afraid of the light." Why are we afraid of the light? The light exposes what we don't want to think about. We assume if we don't think about it, we won't have to deal with it. We tell ourselves we aren't aware of any deep-rooted sin, yet we also don't want to shine God's truth and light onto our hearts to find out anything different.

1 Corinthians 4:4-5 says,

> "For I am not aware of anything against myself, but I am not thereby acquitted. It is the Lord who judges me. Therefore do not pronounce judgment before the time, before the Lord comes, who will bring to light the things now hidden in darkness and will disclose the purposes of the heart. Then each one will receive his commendation from God. For God, who said, 'Let light shine out of darkness,' has shone in our hearts to give the light of the knowledge of the glory of God in the face of Jesus Christ."

God knows the purposes in our hearts that we aren't even aware of. Our conscience may be clear, but that doesn't mean we are innocent. Even if we aren't conscious of them, God will hold us accountable for not dealing with what's inside. Seth Adam Smith once said, "You cannot defeat darkness by running from it, nor can you conquer your inner demons by hiding them from the world. To defeat the darkness, you must bring it into the light."

Ignoring our hearts doesn't protect us from His judgment or accountability. The NLT puts part of the verse this way, "For he will bring our darkest secrets to light and will reveal our private motives." God exposes the motives in our hearts. Exposure means all that is inside of us is uncovered and revealed. In photography, exposure to light is essential to get a bright enough picture to see the details. The less exposure a photo has, the darker the image appears. The less exposure we give God's light into our hearts, the darker our hearts will remain.

When we choose not to fear God's light that will expose our sin, we can see more clearly how to live for God's glory. Paul encourages us in Ephesians 5:8-14 to wake up from our denial. We need to stop acting dead and allow Christ to shine on us and through us. We cannot be a light to the world when we do not let Christ shine in us fully.

> "For at one time you were darkness, but now you are light in the Lord. Walk as children of light *(for the fruit of light is found in all that is good and right and true)*, and try to discern what is pleasing to the Lord. Take no part in the unfruitful works of darkness, but instead expose them. For it is shameful even to speak of the things that they do in secret. But when anything is exposed by the light, it becomes visible, for anything that becomes visible is light. Therefore it says, "Awake, O sleeper, and arise from the dead, and Christ will shine on you."

Sometimes we try to work on our hearts without God or others' help. But inevitably, we will always fail and feel defeated. That is because, as Dr. Martin Luther King Jr. put it, "Darkness cannot drive out darkness: only light can do that." We walk in the light by openly allowing the Lord and others to expose the sin in our hearts. When we invite others to graciously hold us accountable to areas we know we need to grow in, we will have a deeper relationship with them and be more motivated to not live in denial or darkness.

1 John 1:7 says,

> "But if we walk in the light, as he is in the light, we have fellowship with one another, and the blood of Jesus his Son cleanses us from all sin."

Not only does walking in the light free us from the darkness, but it also creates real intimacy with others because we are fully known *(all of our good and all of our bad)* and fully loved without judgment. Growing in community is one of the best ways to be transformed from the inside out.

> "The light shines in the darkness, and the darkness has not overcome it." -John 1:5

> "Again Jesus spoke to them saying, 'I am the light of the world. Whoever follows me will not walk in darkness, but will have the light of life." -John 8:12

> "So Jesus said to them, "The light is among you for a little while longer. Walk while you have the light, lest darkness overtake you. The one who walks in the darkness does not know where he is going. While you have the light, believe in the light, that you may become sons of light." When Jesus had said these things, he departed and hid himself from them." -John 12:35-36

TAKE A MOMENT

1. What seems scary about opening up to another Christian about your struggles within your heart? Why might it be worth the risk?

2. How badly do you want to live in the light so that you can experience the freedom of Christ? What is your next step to do this?

> *Heavenly Father, help me to walk in Your light and not live in the darkness of denial. Help me to wake up from being apathetic about areas I need to change and invite You and others to speak into these areas of my heart. Help me to know who to trust to share my deeper struggles with. I want to live in fellowship with You and others in such a way that I feel known and loved as I am on this journey of being transformed from the inside out. Amen.*

DAY 7
HEALTHY FEAR

Is there such thing as healthy fear? Most certainly. Fear is an automatic and realistic response to a perceived danger. When we are camping and hear growling around the camp, it is healthy to fear there might be a bear near the tent. When we go to the doctor and learn that our heart is unhealthy because our waistline is too large, we can gain a healthy fear that motivates us to eat better, exercise more, and lose weight.

Healthy fears are innately in us so that we can be protected. God's greatest desire is to protect us from destruction and, ultimately, eternal death separated from Him. For us to experience His protection, we must fear Him.

Proverbs 19:23 says,

> "The fear of the Lord leads to life, and whoever has it rests satisfied; he will not be visited by harm."

Unfortunately, we live in a culture where it is practically unheard of for people to fear authority. We are encouraged to question authority instead of trusting they have our best interests in mind. With God, we don't need to question. He's displayed His steadfast love by having Jesus die for us. He's demonstrated His faithfulness by graciously forgiving us when we ask. Sadly, knowing we are loved and forgiven by God isn't always enough for us to obey Him.

We will start to honor, revere, respect, and appropriately fear Him when we remember that He is a holy, righteous God that cannot tolerate sin; when we recognize that every sin deserves death and separation from Him; and when we understand that we are only good because He helps us to be good.

Proverbs 16:6 says,

> "By steadfast love and faithfulness iniquity is atoned for, and by the fear of the Lord one turns away from evil."

He is a just God, and we should never forget how much He abhors sin and the wickedness that is still deep in our hearts.

Psalm 36:1 says,

> "Transgression speaks to the wicked deep in his heart; there is no fear of God before his eyes."

Do we understand the "fear of the Lord" in such a way that we are motivated to obey?

Without a healthy fear of God, we will do what is right in our own eyes, not what God asks us to do. A healthy fear leads us to joyful obedience.

Deuteronomy 5:29 says,

> "Oh that they had such a heart as this always, to fear me and to keep all my commandments, that it might go well with them and with their descendants forever!"

When we fear God, we find wisdom, hate evil, and obey His commands, leading to a joy-filled, satisfying, long life. We will experience safety from sin and its inevitable consequences. Our healthy fear of God will keep us humble, teachable, and growing in our desire to become more like Jesus in our holiness.

2 Corinthians 7:1 says,

> "Since we have these promises, beloved, let us cleanse ourselves from every defilement of body and spirit, bringing holiness to completion in the fear of God."

Fearing God is connected to pursuing holiness to its completion.

Fear leads us to either action or inaction. God wants us to fear Him, not so that we freeze up in terror, overwhelmed that any decision we make may be the wrong one, but so that we fear Him in a way that causes us to want to submit to His commands and obey. There is peace in front of a holy God when we know we are walking in His ways. Fearing God means having such a reverence for Him that it has a significant impact on the way we live our lives. We respect Him, obey Him, submit to His discipline, and worship Him in awe.

Everyone is to fear God, but the fear of God means something different for non-believers than believers. If we are not followers of Jesus and have not accepted Jesus as our Lord and Savior, we must fear God's eternal punishment to pay for our sins. The non-believer will experience the wrath of God. The believer does not need to fear God's wrath because it was placed on Jesus on the cross. We are under the grace of God, yet we are still called to fear God so that we continue to walk in His ways when our flesh is enticing us to do otherwise. Fearing God is crucial if we want to purge sin from our lives and transform from the inside out.

> "Then hear in heaven your dwelling place and forgive and act and render to each whose heart you know, according to all his ways *(for you, you only, know the hearts of all the children of mankind)*, that they may fear you all the days that they live in the land that you gave to our fathers."
> -1 Kings 8:39-40

> "I will make with them an everlasting covenant, that I will not turn away from doing good to them. And I will put the fear of me in their hearts, that they may not turn from me."
> -Jeremiah 32:40

“If you will not listen, if you will not take it to heart to give honor to my name, says the Lord of hosts, then I will send the curse upon you and I will curse your blessings. Indeed, I have already cursed them because you do not lay it to heart.” -Malachi 2:2

“So the church throughout all Judea and Galilee and Samaria had peace and was being built up. And walking in the fear of the Lord and in the comfort of the Holy Spirit, it multiplied.” -Acts 9:31

“Now then, let fear of the Lord be upon you. Be careful what you do, for there is no injustice with the Lord our God, or partiality or taking bribes.” -2 Chronicles 19:7

“And he said to man, ‘Behold, the fear of the Lord, that is wisdom, and to turn away from evil is understanding.’” -Job 28:28

“The fear of the Lord is the beginning of wisdom, and the knowledge of the Holy One is insight.” -Proverbs 9:10

“The fear of the Lord is a fountain of life, that one may turn away from the snares of death.” -Proverbs 14:27

TAKE A MOMENT

1. How can fearing the Lord lead you to obedience? What are the consequences if we don't fear the Lord?

2. What areas of your life do you need to fear the Lord in more?

> *Heavenly Father, You are holy and just. I do not deserve Your grace and mercy. I deserve Your wrath and judgment. Thank You that because of Jesus' death on the cross, I do not need to fear Your wrath. Lord, help me have a healthy fear of You to obey You and not my flesh. Help me transform from the inside out by understanding that fearing You leads to wisdom, obedience, peace, and joy. Amen.*

DAY 8
SEEKING INTIMACY

God made us for relationships. We are not meant to live in isolation. We are relational beings that need deep intimacy to have great joy and fulfillment. But people fail us. People abandon us. People abuse us. People disappoint us. When this happens, we start to pull away, not trusting people have our best interests in mind. We don't feel safe.

We live in a fallen world where each person we engage with is fallible and imperfect. Yet we are still called to live in community, love deeply, and emotionally engage with others. How can our hearts do that when we know we may get hurt?

When we long for intimacy, do we seek people first or the Lord? When we have a deep intimate relationship with God first, we can have deeper relationships with the imperfect people around us. In our relationship with God, we find the greatest security because He never leaves us or abandons us. He guides us and protects us. He comforts us in ways no human can. He inspires hope in ways no one else can promise. He delivers peace in the fiercest storms. When we have intimacy with the Lord, knowing He provides these things for us, we can grow in intimacy with the people around us. When we don't depend on others for our needs, we can enjoy what people can give us, and relationships can deepen.

Jeremiah 29:13 gives us this promise from God,

> "You will seek me and find me, when you seek me with all your heart."

God promises that when we seek Him by going to Him in prayer and reading His Word, we will find Him. It is not about checking off another devotional in the morning but truly stopping to seek God with our hearts. When we choose to take the time to seek a relationship with God before we engage with the people around us, our hearts rejoice with joy from being in His presence. We have satisfying rest no matter the circumstances around us. Our hearts revive with new strength. When we have this revived, rested, rejoicing heart, we can genuinely enjoy intimacy with others around us because we are already filled up with the fullness of God.

When we seek God, we focus on who He is and all of His attributes. God is all-powerful. God is in control. God is holy and just. God is loving and merciful. When we meditate on who He is, we bring Him glory, and our hearts rejoice!

1 Chronicles 16:10 says,

> "Glory in his holy name; let the hearts of those who seek the Lord rejoice!"

When we seek God, knowing He has a plan and purpose for us, He will give us rest in all aspects of our lives. Rest in our families. Rest in our friendships. Rest in our finances. Rest in our futures.

2 Chronicles 15:15 says,

> "And all Judah rejoiced over the oath, for they had sworn with all their heart and had sought him with their whole desire, and he was found by them, and the Lord gave them rest all around."

When we seek God humbly, He will bring new strength into our lives to walk through whatever are our current circumstances with a new vision, clearer purpose, and a greater resolve to persevere with hope.

Psalm 69:32 says,

> "When the humble see it they will be glad; you who seek God, let your hearts revive."

Seeking real intimacy begins by seeking God. When we experience God, our hearts are transformed from the inside out, and we will be able to enjoy intimacy with others deeply. This is because we come with already filled, healthy hearts in our relationships with others.

> "But from there you will seek the Lord your God and you will find him, if you search after him with all your heart and with all your soul." -Deuteronomy 4:29

> "And those who had set their hearts to seek the Lord God of Israel came after them from all the tribes of Israel to Jerusalem to sacrifice to the Lord, the God of their fathers." -2 Chronicles 11:16

TAKE A MOMENT

1. What will we find if we seek God with all of our hearts?

2. How will seeking God first bring us the intimacy we need?

> *Heavenly Father, "You have said, "Seek my face." My heart says to you, "Your face, Lord do I seek" (Psalm 27:8). I come expectant to seek You and all of who You are. May I meditate on Your attributes in such a way that I experience your intimate presence. May my heart rejoice in who You are. May I find rest in You no matter what is happening around me. May You revive my heart with Your strength so that I can pursue others. I want to have healthy intimacy in the friendships around me because you already fill me. Amen.*

DAY 9
WORD VIEW VS. WORLDVIEW

Our hearts are easily impressionable. Have you ever watched or read a love story where a person is in a marriage where the spouse doesn't seem to give them the time of day? They are this wonderful person, but unseen and not cherished by the spouse. Then, an intriguing coworker comes along, and a spark leads to a "business" lunch, which leads to a night in a bedroom. We watch it thinking, "I'm so happy they are now in a relationship where they are loved and valued." We don't even think about the fact they had an affair. The affair becomes justified in our minds because the spouse wasn't giving them enough time and attention. These thoughts affect what we believe. What we believe, we start to live out. We flirt with a person at work, thinking it's just fun and games. We start texting them about personal things because they seem to understand and care about us. We dream what life might be like if we were married to them. And an affair can be right around the corner. Our hearts are easily impressionable.

We cannot call ourselves followers of Jesus and follow our hearts. Remember, our hearts deceive us. How many times have we heard people say when it comes to relationships, "Just follow your heart?" When we do that, we are at risk of no longer following the commands of the Lord found in the Bible. We follow what feels right, what society encourages is acceptable, and our hearts fall into sin.

Numbers 15:39 says,

> "And it shall be a tassel for you to look at and remember all the commandments of the Lord, to do them, not to follow after your own heart and your own eyes, which you are inclined to whore after."

We live in a post-Christian society. A society that no longer respects or values the clear principles found in the Bible. The world says that certain things done to us are unforgivable. The Word says to forgive anyone for anything because Christ has done the same with us. The world says that marriage's ultimate goal is to be happy and satisfied, and if we are not, we can divorce. The Word says that we should not get divorced but if we do, only if there is an affair. The world says that the end justifies the means. The Word says that having integrity in the process matters. The world says that it is our bodies, so we can choose what to do with them. The Word says that our bodies are not our own because we were paid for with a price, Christ's death. It's convicting to see the contrast between what we wish was right and what the Bible actually says is right. Our hearts have already been enticed.

Listen to what Jeremiah 13:10 says about this,

> "This evil people, who refuse to hear my words, who stubbornly follow their own heart have gone after other gods to serve them and worship them, shall be like this loincloth, which is good for nothing."

Our Christian faith is good for nothing if we chose to say we are Christians but don't change our worldview to be Biblical. We are no different from the world because we follow our hearts just like they do.

What we believe becomes the driving force behind our emotions, decisions, and actions. If what we think about something cannot be supported by Scripture, we must humbly consider if it is a wrong belief. Every culture, every society has unbiblical worldviews that must be challenged and transformed by the truth of Scripture. We must be careful that we are not taken "captive through hollow and deceptive philosophy, which depends on human tradition and the basic principles of this world rather than on Christ" *(Colossians 2:8)*. We may not be able to change the laws of the land, but we can change how we abide by the laws of the Scriptures. When we have the Bible as our foundation for making decisions on what we say and do, we will not follow our hearts, which seduce us to live in what feels good at the moment. To transform from the inside out, we must stop following our hearts and follow Scripture instead.

> "Do not conform any longer to the pattern of this world, but be transformed by the renewing of your mind."
> -Romans 12:2

TAKE A MOMENT

1. What worldview have you been living out that is unbiblical?

2. What can you do to make sure that your beliefs and actions are Biblical?

> *Heavenly Father, thank You for Your Word that guides me on what I should believe and why. Help me to not live by the values of the culture, but to live by the values in Your Word instead. Reveal to me where I have faulty beliefs or values so that I change from the inside out. Help me not to follow my heart but to follow Your Word instead. Amen.*

DAY 10
PREPARE FOR RAIN

Rain. It's cold, damp, and can be destructive. Rain causes accidents on the roads, flooding in the valleys and makes us shiver to the bone. Rain hinders our visibility and hides the sun. It is gloomy and can sometimes even affect our mood. When it rains, it often pours.

We've heard the saying, "Prepare for a rainy day." This means saving up money, food, or resources when the storms in life hit. We never know when a time of trouble will come, but we can try to prepare as much as possible. When we store up what we need, we can make it through any storm. We keep what we've stored up in a special place that we know we can draw from when needed. We do this not because we are fearful but because we are responsible for doing what we can to be equipped for whatever is to come our way.

Rainy days come in our hearts as well. These are the days where sadness overwhelms us, and the tears won't stop. The days we react in an ungodly manner and see the destruction in the relationships around us, feeling defeated. The days we give into foolishness and can't seem to backpedal our way out of a decision. We weren't ready for the rain of emotions, the rain of temptations, the rain of the pressures of life, and now, we feel stuck in them.

When we don't prepare for the storms in life, we usually turn to sin-filled solutions rather than soul-filling solutions. When we don't save up for house repairs, and our roof begins to leak, we get into debt to repair it. When we see someone is upset with us, we fight back with defensiveness and anger, rather than humbly listening and learning how we've affected the other person. When there is a sudden illness or death of a loved one, we may run from God, wondering how He could be a loving God and allow this to happen. Storms increase our stress, cause struggles in our relationships, and may strain our relationship with God. This is why we must prepare for the rain. Storms will come, but are we ready?

What do we need to store up to be ready?

Psalm 119:11 says,

> "I have stored up your word in my heart, that I might not sin against you."

Our most incredible resource to help us wade through any storm is God's Word. When we take the time to read His Words during times we are not in a storm, we will remember them when we are in a storm. God's Word gives us wisdom on what to do and how to respond.

> "Your word is a lamp to my feet and a light to my path." -Psalm 119:105

God's Word gives us comfort and the courage to press on.

> "My soul melts away for sorrow; strengthen me according to your word!" -Psalm 119:28

God's Word also guides us on how not to sin when times get challenging, and we feel we are about to lose self-control.

> "How can a young man keep his way pure? By guarding it according to your word." -Psalm 119:9

We can walk through storms with hope, knowing God is the God of rainbows and keeps His promises. God is the God of new growth after the rain. God is the God that can rebuild, restore and renew places long devastated in our lives. We store up God's Word now so that His words come to our mind when we need them.

Many Christians around the Word live in countries where it is illegal to have a Bible or be a Christ-follower. These believers memorize entire books of the Bible.

They understand Psalm 119:114,

> "You are my hiding place and my shield; I hope in your word."

When they are prisoners for their faith, God's Word reminds them to be hopeful and still worship God in their dire circumstances.

If we want to start building healthy hearts that can navigate the storms of life, we must be reading, meditating, and memorizing God's Word. We need it at our disposal so that our hearts don't deceive us in the storm. God's Word will prepare us to be strong from the inside out, and we will come out of trials victorious!

> "For Ezra had set his heart to study the Law of the Lord, and to do it and to teach his statues and rules in Israel." -Ezra 7:10

> "As for that in the good soil, they are those who, hearing the word, hold it fast in an honest and good heart, and bear fruit with patience." -Luke 8:15

> "My soul clings to the dust; give me life according to your word!" -Psalm 119:25

TAKE A MOMENT

1. What topic in the Bible would you like to study to help you prepare for future storms or a storm you are currently experiencing? i.e., peace, hope, comfort, obedience, etc.

2. Go to blueletterbible.org. Type in that word or topic. Every verse in the Bible with that word will be listed. Read the verses and choose which ones to memorize.

> *Heavenly Father, thank You for Your Word that can give me wisdom, comfort, direction, and hope in my greatest storms in life. Set my heart to study Your Word so that I will do what it says in times of trials. May I hold fast to Your Word so that my life will bear fruit as I walk in the storm with patience and trust in You. Thank You for transforming me from the inside out with Your Living Word. Amen.*

DAY 11
HOLY-MUZZLE

What we say matters. One "no" can break someone's heart. One lie can lose someone's trust. One disrespectful word, and we devalue a person. Words slip out, causing damage to others we can't quickly fix. Sometimes, our mouths just need a serious spanking! Unfortunately, all that would do is give us a fat lip.

For us to get our mouths to stop gossiping, slandering, lying and cursing, we need to know the source. Our words come from the health of our hearts.

Luke 6:45 says,

> "The good person out of the good treasure of his heart produces good, and the evil person out of his evil treasure produces evil, for out of the abundance of the heart his mouth speaks."

Our hearts are either full of goodness, which overflows with words of kindness, grace, love and encouragement, or our hearts are full of evil, which overflows with words leading to conflict, hurt and condemnation.

The saying, "Think before you speak," seems like good advice, but it's faulty. Sometimes we do think before we speak and still say ungodly things. Are we building others up by noticing what they are doing right? Or do we tear them down with criticism assuming that will convict them to change? Are we building bridges to the gospel by not taking a personal offense with someone who believes differently than us? Or are we hypocrites to the outside world who sees we aren't able to give others grace and love?

James 1:26 says,

> "If anyone thinks he is religious and does not bridle his tongue but deceives his heart, this person's religion is worthless."

We have no influence or witness to the non-believing world if we don't learn how to bridle our tongue.

The word, bridal, means to restrain or control. We bridle horses so that they obey and go in the proper direction. When we bridle our tongues, our life and relationships will go in a better direction. So, how do we do that? We pause our words, thoughts and emotions to put on, what I like to call, a holy muzzle. Our mouths should not speak until God's holiness covers them. When we are sure that what we are about to say will glorify God and help others, we can talk.

Colossians 4:6 commands,

> "Let your speech always be gracious, seasoned with salt, so that you may know how you ought to answer each person."

It continues in Colossians 8:8,

> "But now you must put them all away: anger, wrath, malice, slander, and obscene talk from your mouth."

And Ephesians 4:29 says,

> "Let no corrupting talk come out of your mouths, but only such as is good for building up, as fits the occasion, that it may give grace to those who hear."

When we pause to put on our holy muzzle, we take a moment to ask God to give us love and self-control in our response. We ask for His wisdom on what to say, when to say it, and how. We ask for our mouths to bring healing and not further hurt.

Proverbs 12:18 says,

> "There is one whose rash words are like sword thrusts, but the tongue of the wise brings healing."

We want to put away our fighting words and put on words of reconciliation and restoration.

What we say matters. Our words bring life or death to the relationships around us. Let us be those who wear a holy muzzle, pausing to pray for God's words and wisdom. This is how we transform our hearts from the inside out and bring healing and hope to those around us.

> "Everyone utters lies to his neighbor, with flattering lips and a double heart they speak." -Psalm 12:2
>
> "You brood of vipers! How can you speak good, when you are evil? For out of the abundance of the heart the mouth speaks." -Matthew 12:34
>
> "But what comes out of the mouth proceeds from the heart, and this defiles a person." -Matthew 15:18
>
> "When words are many, transgression is not lacking, but whoever restrains his lips is prudent." -Proverbs 10:19
>
> "Death and life are in the power of the tongue, and those who love it will eat its fruits." -Proverbs 18:21
>
> "For lack of wood the fire goes out, and where there is no whisper, quarreling ceases." -Proverbs 26:20
>
> "I tell you, on the day of judgment people will give account for every careless word they speak." -Matthew 12:36

“If we put bits into the mouths of horses so that they obey us, we guide their whole bodies as well. Look at the ships also: though they are so large and are driven by strong winds, they are guided by a very small ruder wherever the will of the pilot directs. So also the tongue is a small member, yet it boasts of great things. How great a forest is set ablaze by such a small fire! And the tongue is a fire, a world of unrighteousness. The tongue is set among our members, staining the whole body, setting on fire the entire course of life, and set on fire by hell. For every kind of beast and bird, of reptile and sea creature, can be tamed and has been tamed by mankind, but no human being can tame the tongue. It is a restless evil, full of deadly poison. With it we bless our Lord and Father, and with it we curse people who are made in the likeness of God. From the same mouth comes blessing and cursing. My brothers, these things ought not to be so.” -James 3:3-11

TAKE A MOMENT

1. What do you need to change in how you speak to others?

2. How can you remind yourself to put on your holy muzzle to make sure you are speaking words that bring healing?

> *Heavenly Father, let the words of my mouth and the meditation of my heart be acceptable in Your sight, O Lord, my Rock and my Redeemer (Psalm 19:14). Please help me to pause before I speak. Give me Your words and wisdom to bring healing and hope to those around me. Show me that there is a blessing in it for me and others when I restrain my tongue. Transform my heart by changing what I say and how I say it. I allow You to bridle my tongue so that I can speak only as You want me to speak. Amen.*

DAY 12

STUBBORN HEART → TEACHABLE HEART

For the past 11 days, we have been exploring the truth that we cannot trust our hearts and that we must humbly admit that we need God's help to see what is going on inside of us. For the next 27 days, we will study specific characteristics of the heart defined in the Bible to honestly examine how we need to transform our hearts. Now the real heart surgery begins. We will take time to pause, reflect, and ask God to reveal what He sees in our hearts when it comes to these heart characteristics. Then we can purge out the unhealthy parts of our hearts to pursue the characteristics of a healthy heart.

Today, we will begin by studying the stubborn heart vs. the teachable heart. Our hearts are either one or the other when it comes to God, His Word, and listening to others who have our best interests in mind. Let's dig in.

If we have a stubborn heart, we are determined not to change our attitudes, positions, or opinions on things, even if there are good reasons to do so. We aren't humble. We don't read the Bible to learn. We don't ask questions about what we believe and check if it aligns with what Scripture teaches. We don't seek counsel to make Biblically wise decisions. We have a hard time receiving correction or criticism without resentment or retaliation. We don't want to be wrong or have to change.

How do we know if stubbornness is rooted in our hearts? Think about who's advice you are open to hearing. Will you submit to the Bible's commands, or do you instead follow your own wisdom, or worse yet, the world's? We get pregnant, and the world says, "Have an abortion. You're not ready. A baby will mess up your plans. It's easier." We get in debt with our uncontrolled spending, and the world says, "It doesn't matter. Get another credit card." We are in a relationship but not yet married and think, "How can it be wrong to be intimate when I love him or her? It feels right, so it must be right."

Jeremiah 7:24 says,

> "But they did not obey or incline their ear, but walked in their own counsels and the stubbornness of their evil hearts, and went backward and not forward."

Our stubbornness leads us backward in our faith, not forwards. We give in to temptations that become stumbling blocks, not stepping stones to move forward in our faith. If we maintain a stubborn heart, God will at some point stop convicting us and allow us to follow our wisdom instead of His.

Psalm 81:12 says,

> "So I gave them over to their stubborn hearts, to follow their own counsels."

If we have a teachable heart, we are eager to learn what the Bible says. We are aware we have limited knowledge and need to continue to learn and ask for guidance. We will let go of previous unbiblical beliefs and be humble enough to admit we were wrong. We are willing to change our views and practices in light of what we learn in the Bible. When our hearts are open to learning, we can receive wisdom from God and others.

Psalm 51:6 says,

> "Behold, you delight in truth in the inward being, and you teach me wisdom in the secret heart."

We strive to grow in having a Biblical mindset. We ask for feedback, and we respond well to it. We can receive truth and apply it, transforming our hearts from unhealthy to healthy.

Proverbs 4:4 says,

> "He taught me and said to me, 'Let your heart hold fast to my words; keep my commandments, and live.'"

Inside Out

To be transformed from the inside out, we must have teachable hearts.

"But they say, 'That is in vain! We will follow our own plans, and will everyone act according to the stubbornness of his evil heart.'" -Jeremiah 18:12

"And he said to them, 'You are those who justify yourselves before men, but God knows your hearts. For what is exalted among men is an abomination in the sight of God.'" -Luke 16:15

"And you say, 'How I hate discipline, and my heart despised reproof!'" -Proverbs 5:12

"But because of your hard and impenitent heart you are storing up wrath for yourself on the day of wrath when God's righteous judgment will be revealed." -Romans 2:5

"I do not turn aside from your rules, for you have taught me." -Psalm 119:102

"Give instruction to a wise man, and he will be still wiser; teach a righteous man, and he will increase in learning." -Proverbs 9:9

TAKE A MOMENT

1. What traces do you see of a stubborn heart in yourself?

2. How can you be intentional to grow in having a teachable heart?

> *Heavenly Father, I want to have a teachable heart. "Teach me, and I will be silent; make me understand how I have gone astray" (Job 6:24). I sit here listening for You to bring areas to mind where I have been stubborn. "Teach me your way, O Lord, that I may walk in your truth; unite my heart to fear your name" (Psalm 86:11). "Put false ways far from me and graciously teach me your law" (Psalm 119:29). "Make me to know your ways, O Lord; teach me your paths. Lead me in your truth and teach me, for you are the God of my salvation; for you I wait all the day long" (Psalm 25:4-5). "Teach me to do your will, for you are my God! Let your Spirit lead me on level ground" (Psalm 143:10)! "Teach me, O Lord, the way of your statutes; and I will keep it to the end" (Psalm 119:33). Lord, purge stubbornness out of me and fill me with Your truth so that I can humbly change my ways and become more like You. Amen.*

DAY 13

FORGETFUL HEART → REMEMBERING HEART

Remembering is a powerful thing. We can remember joyful, momentous occasions, which lead to feeling motivated, hopeful and loved. We can also remember horrific tragedies where we feel grief, fear, anger, and hopelessness. We can recall them over and over again, reliving them as if they were yesterday. The more we relive something through remembering, the easier it is to remember it in the future. This can work for us or against us when it comes to our hearts' health. What we choose to focus on and remember matters.

God is there in the cherished moments of our lives, and God is there in the darkest valleys. This is reality. The question is, "Do we remember who God is when we are remembering our past, or have we forgotten His presence in our lives?"

When life is going well, and we see success, and have little concerns in life, we may not remember God. We may forget all that He has done to bless us. We may stop reading the Bible, stop praying and stop gathering with other believers because we don't feel a need for God. Instead of enjoying the blessings of life with God, we take His blessings and forget that it all comes from Him.

Hosea 13:6 shows us this reality,

> "But when they had grazed, they became full, they were filled, and their heart was lifted up; therefore they forgot me."

When we feel satisfied by this world's comforts, we can easily forget that God blessed us with those comforts. Deuteronomy 8:18 encourages us that when life is going well,

> "You shall remember the LORD your God, for it is he who gives you power to get wealth, that he may confirm his covenant that he swore to your fathers, as it is this day."

We forget the faithfulness of God. We forget how He has provided for us. We forget how He has protected us. We forget how He has pursued us, forgiven us, and empowered us with His Spirit. We forget He has a plan for our lives. We forget that the power and wealth He's given us is to further His Kingdom and not our own.

Deuteronomy 4:9 says,

> "Only take care, and keep your soul diligently, lest you forget the things that your eyes have seen, and lest they depart from your heart all the days of your life. Make them known to your children and your children's children."

We are to share with those following after us how we have seen God work in our lives. This reminds us and motivates them to trust God as trials begin to come in their own lives. We are to remember who God is, what He has done, and what He promises to do in the future.

> "And now I am about to go the way of all the earth, and you know in your hearts and souls, all of you, that not one word has failed of all the good things that the Lord your God promised concerning you. All have come to pass for you; not one of them has failed." -Joshua 23:14

We are to hear stories from those who have gone before us to remember who God is.

> "Remember the days of old; consider the years of many generations; ask your father, and he will show you, your elders, and they will tell you." -Deuteronomy 32:7

When we think about our day, our thoughts should meditate first on God and His faithfulness, not the failures of today or the worries of tomorrow.

Psalm 63:5-7 says,

> "My soul will be satisfied as with fat and rich food, and my mouth will praise you with joyful lips, when I remember you upon my bed, and meditate on you in the watches of the night; for you have been my help, and in the shadow of your wings I will sing for joy."

What we remember matters. Let us focus our hearts on remembering what is true about God and stop focusing on what should have happened, what could have happened, or what did happen. Then we can have praise on our lips and joy in our hearts, not because of what has happened, but because of who God is despite what has occurred. Remember who God is will transform our hearts from the inside out in any situation.

> "Remember the wondrous works that he has done, his miracles and the judgments he uttered." -1 Chronicles 16:12

> "I said, "Let me remember my song in the night; let me meditate in my heart." Then my spirit made a diligent search: "Will the Lord spurn forever, and never again be favorable? Has his steadfast love forever ceased? Are his promises at an end for all time? Has God forgotten to be gracious? Has he in anger shut up his compassion?" Then I said, "I will appeal to this, to the years of the right hand of the Most High." I will remember the deeds of the LORD; yes, I will remember your wonders of old. I will ponder all your work, and meditate on your mighty deeds. Your way, O God, is holy. What god is great like our God? You are the God who works wonders; you

have made known your might among the peoples. You with your arm redeemed your people, the children of Jacob and Joseph." -Psalm 77:6-15

"I remember the days of old; I meditate on all that you have done; I ponder the work of your hands." -Psalm 143:5

"Remember the former things of old; for I am God, and there is no other; I am God, and there is none like me." -Isaiah 46:9

"Whom did you dread and fear, so that you lied, and did not remember me, did not lay it to heart? Have I not held my peace, even for a long time, and you do not fear me?" -Isaiah 57:11

"Remember, then, what you received and heard. Keep it, and repent. If you will not wake up, I will come like a thief, and you will not know at what hour I will come against you." -Revelation 3:3

TAKE A MOMENT

1. When life is going well, how can remembering who God is help you to use your blessings to further His Kingdom and not yours?

2. When life is challenging, how can remembering who God is help you to have an eternal perspective and not focus only on your temporal circumstances?

> *Heavenly Father, please help me to remember You in the times of blessing and the times of trials. Help me focus on who You are rather than the circumstances around me. May I not forget that You are present in every situation. May I remember You are faithful. May I remember the stories of old how You provided and protected Your people, believing in my heart that You will do the same with me. I know that remembering You will transform my heart no matter my situation. Amen.*

DAY 14

QUESTIONING HEART → TRUSTING HEART

Life happens. We lose our job. Our house goes into foreclosure. Our spouse is unfaithful. Our children rebel. Our family member gets a terminal illness. It is in these critical moments of pain and loss that our hearts may question God's intentions toward us. Does He care? Where is He? How can this be part of His plan? What good can come out of this? If these questions remained unanswered, they can lead to significant doubts about who God is and if we should trust Him. We have a preconceived idea of what we think God should be like. If He doesn't fit into our opinion of what we think is acceptable, we start to question His love and loyalty to us.

Jesus knows when we question Him in our hearts. He knew that the scribes and Pharisees wondered how He could forgive a man of his sin in Luke 5:22.

> "When Jesus perceived their thoughts, he answered them, 'Why do you question in your hearts?'"

It should have blown them away that Jesus not only forgave sins but knew what they were thinking in their hearts! Who can know our thoughts except for God? He was showing them more of who He was to encourage them to believe He indeed was the Son of God who has the authority to forgive sins.

Jesus knew that His disciples questioned if He had risen from the dead. When they saw Him, they were startled and frightened.

> "He said to them, 'Why are you troubled, and why do doubts arise in your hearts?'" -Luke 24:38

He showed them His nail-scarred hands and feet, yet some still didn't believe it was Him. It was only after He reminded them what was written about Himself in the Old Testament that their hearts stopped questioning Him.

Proverbs 3:5 says we are to,

> "Trust in the Lord with all your heart, and do not lean on your own understanding."

God will not always make sense to us. To grow in trusting Him with our whole hearts, we must stop trusting our assumptions about who we think He should be and saturate ourselves with the Word of God. We can begin by reading John's book and studying Jesus' life. There are seven "I am" statements in the book of John that Jesus uses to describe Himself. These statements are given to us to help us know Him and trust Him more.

> "I am the Bread of Life." -John 6:35

Jesus will sustain and satisfy our deepest needs emotionally, physically and financially.

> "I am the light of the World." -John 8:13

He will help us out of the darkness of sin and walk into the light of life to experience freedom.

> "I am the door to salvation." -John 10:9

When we invite Jesus into our lives, we have eternal security knowing we are adopted into His family and He will never abandon us.

> "I am the Good Shepherd." -John 10:11,14

He wants to guide and protect us on our journey through life.

> "I am the Resurrection and the Life." -John 11:25

Death had no power over Him. We, too, will be resurrected when Jesus returns and have eternal life with Him. We do not need to fear death.

> "I am the way, the truth and the life." -John 14:6

Jesus is the only way for us to have a relationship with God the Father. He is the only truth. He is the only One who can bring us abundant life.

> "I am the vine, and you are the branches." -John 15:1, 5

We abide in Jesus to bear fruit in our lives and have an abundant life.

Our faith increases when trust is built by learning Jesus' character and seeing how it is consistent throughout Scripture.

> "So faith comes from hearing, and hearing through the word of Christ." -Romans 10:17

God wants us to pour our hearts out to Him when life gets confusing and complicated. He wants to be our refuge of safety during those times.

Psalm 62:8 says,

> "Trust in him at all times, O people; pour out your heart before him; God is a refuge for us."

Jesus becomes our refuge when we cast our burdens onto Him. He will help us carry the uncertainties of life so that we do not live in hopelessness and despair. We just need to take the time to get to know Him better, trust Him more, and rest in who He is. Life happens, but with a trusting heart, we will rest in Him from the inside out.

> "Now some of the scribes were sitting there, questioning in their hearts, 'Why does this man speak like that? He is blaspheming! Who can forgive sins but God alone?' And immediately Jesus, perceiving in his spirit that they thus questioned within themselves said to them, 'Why do you question these things in your heart?'" -Mark 2:6-8

“The Lord is my strength and my shield; in him my heart trusts, and I am helped; my heart exults, and with my song I give thanks to him.” -Psalm 28:7

“For our heart is glad in him, because we trust in his holy name.” -Psalm 33:21

“He is not afraid of bad news; his heart is firm, trusting in the Lord.” -Psalm 112:7

TAKE A MOMENT

1. How does studying God's character help us grow in our trust in Him?
2. What are areas that are challenging for you to trust God?

> *Heavenly Father, help me trust You when I can't make sense of the world. I do not want to lean on my own understanding, but to trust that Your ways are higher than my ways and Your thoughts are higher than my thoughts. Help me to learn who You are by reading Your Word. Help me to believe You love me, You are in control, You are faithful, and You have a plan and purpose for my life. May my faith increase so that I question You less and trust You more. Transform my heart by trusting in You. Amen.*

DAY 15

UNBELIEVING HEART → BELIEVING HEART

What we believe in our hearts matter. For our hearts to be healthy, we must know what we believe, why we believe it, and that it is a correct belief according to the Bible. Just because we sincerely believe something doesn't mean it's true. Kids sincerely believe in Santa, but it doesn't mean the man at the mall is truly him. Saying we believe in God, or even saying we believe in Jesus, doesn't necessarily lead to salvation.

Many self-acclaimed evangelical Christians now have an unbiblical belief of who Jesus is because relativism and universalism are infiltrating their theology. In a survey taken in 2020 by The State of Theology Group, 52% of Americans believe Jesus was a great teacher but not God. 30% of evangelicals agreed. 25% of evangelicals also are not confident that Jesus' resurrection was a real historical event *(State of American Theology Study, 2014)*. 46% of evangelicals agree that God accepts all religions' worship *(Lifeway Research, 2016)*. 65% of "Christians" believe there are multiple paths to Heaven *(US Religious Landscape Study, 2014)*. 69% of church goers believe that everyone will go to Heaven *(Baylor Religion Survey, 2014)*. 50% of Americans believe Jesus sinned *(Barna Group, 2015)*. 77% of Americans believe personal salvation results from good works *(Lifeway Research, 2016)*. Have our hearts fallen into these false views about Jesus and salvation?

Hebrews 3:12 warns us about this,

> "Take care, brothers, lest there be in any of you an evil, unbelieving heart, leading you to fall away from the living God."

Believing in false theology will slowly cause us to fall away from the one true God.

Our culture wants us to believe that everyone with "a good heart" will go to Heaven. But haven't we already read in great detail that our hearts are evil and no one is good? No one deserves Heaven. Our good intentions are not enough because sin must be paid for. We cannot allow wrong theology to be rooted in our hearts, nor can we dismiss what the Bible teaches.

We are warned about this in Luke 8:12-13,

> "The ones along the path are those who have heard; then the devil comes and takes away the word from their hearts, so that they may not believe and be saved. And the ones on the rock are those who, when they hear the word, receive it with joy. But these have no root; they believe for a while, and in time of testing fall away."

What we believe about Jesus in our hearts matter. What the Bible says about Jesus is what is true. Jesus is God. Jesus never sinned. Jesus could have never been our perfect sacrifice on the cross if He had sinned even once. Jesus did rise from the dead. His resurrection confirms He is God and has power over death, sin, and Satan. God does not accept worship from any religion because He demands that we have no other gods before Him. Not everyone will go to Heaven. There is only one way to get to Heaven, by believing in Jesus as our Lord and Savior. Jesus being our Lord means we surrender our lives to Him and desire to follow Him in what He asks us to do. We understand that it is not our good works that save us, but nor are we saved if our lives do not have surrendered hearts toward Him.

Ephesians 2:8-9 says,

> "For by grace you have been saved through faith. And this is not your own doing; it is the gift of God, not a result of works so that no one may boast."

Our salvation comes by confessing that Jesus is our Lord. We vow to submit and follow what He says according to the Bible. It is also crucial that we believe Jesus rose from the dead because His resurrection is proof He is God. When our hearts believe these truths, we are justified before God. Justified means our sins are cover by Christ's atoning sacrifice, and we are seen as righteous before God.

> "Because, if you confess with your mouth that Jesus is Lord and believe in your heart that God raised him from the dead, you will be saved. For with the heart one believes and is justified, and with the mouth one confesses and is saved." -Romans 10:9-10

John 7:38 says,

> "Whoever believes in me, as the Scripture has said, 'Out of his heart will flow rivers of living water.'"

When we believe what the Bible says about Jesus, our hearts will flow with life from the inside out, and we will experience the joy of our salvation!

> "You believe that God is one; you do well. Even the demons believe-and shudder!" -James 2:19

> "Immediately the father of the child cried out and said, "I believe; help my unbelief!" -Mark 9:24

> "You are my witnesses," declares the LORD, "and my servant whom I have chosen, that you may know and believe me and understand that I am he. Before me no god was formed, nor shall there be any after me." -Isaiah 43:10

“Whoever believes in him is not condemned, but whoever does not believe is condemned already, because he has not believed in the name of the only Son of God.” -John 3:18

“I told you that you would die in your sins, for unless you believe that I am he you will die in your sins.” -John 8:24

“For to this end we toil and strive, because we have our hope set on the living God, who is the Savior of all people, especially of those who believe.” -1 Timothy 4:10

“Though you have not seen him, you love him. Though you do not now see him, you believe in him and rejoice with joy that is inexpressible and filled with glory.” -1 Peter 1:8

“I write these things to you who believe in the name of the Son of God, that you may know that you have eternal life.” -1 John 5:13

TAKE A MOMENT

1. Are there any points mentioned above in which you have unbelief?
2. How can studying who Jesus is in the Bible help you to have your heart rooted in proper theology?

> *Heavenly Father, thank You that You sent Your Son, Jesus, to die on the cross for my sins. Thank You that He was sinless and rose from the dead, conquering sin, Satan, and death. Please help me to never cheapen Jesus' sacrifice by believing wrong theology. May I remember that it is by grace I am saved, not by my good deeds. Show me where my beliefs may not be following Scripture so that my heart can believe what is right and true. Amen.*

DAY 16

COMPLACENT HEART → THANKFUL HEART

If we are lazy in life, our physical hearts will not be strong and healthy. Without intentional exercise and perseverance to care about our health, we will have a slow, steady decline in our physical health. We may overlook the daily impact of complacency, but over time, we feel more lethargic, less excited about movement, and comfier lounging on the couch. We become overly content with the current situation and unconcerned about changing it. This can lead to apathy toward our own needs and others' needs around us.

Complacency happens in our spiritual lives as well. We'd rather watch the action on TV than live the adventure God has for us in real life. We stop reading the Bible. We stop going to church and gathering with other believers. We stop thinking about becoming more like Jesus or how to engage with others around us spiritually. We don't even realize that our laziness is affecting us. We talk to God less, which means we hear from God less. We stop wondering what God is doing in the lives of the people around us. We begin to see God as distant, unengaged, uncaring, and eventually, pointless.

Zephaniah 1:12 warns us how God sees complacent people.

> "At that time I will search Jerusalem with lamps, and I will punish the men who are complacent, those who say in their hearts, 'The Lord will not do good, nor will he do ill.'"

Complacency leads to becoming dull in our faith. We lack interest in God, we lack excitement to do His will, and we become less of a light to the world around us. Dull hearts affect our ability to hear God and see what He is doing around us.

Matthew 13:15 says,

> "For this people's heart has grown dull, and with their ears they can barely hear, and their eyes they have closed, lest they should see with their eyes and hear with their ears and understand with their heart and turn, and I would heal them."

Maybe we still go to church. Maybe we even open our mouths to sing songs. Maybe we say we believe in God, but really, we haven't talked to Him in days or months.

Matthew 15:8 warns about this,

> "This people honors me with their lips, but their heart is far from me."

How do we get out of our complacency? How do we begin caring again for our spiritual health and the health of those around us? It starts by transforming our complacent hearts into thankful hearts. When we are thankful, we understand that we have been given so much by God. We are relieved that we won't have to experience His wrath. When we are thankful toward God, we remember that God is good, faithful, and worthy of heart-felt praise, despite our circumstances.

Being thankful with our whole hearts during challenging moments in life also protects us from other sins like grumbling and complaining.

> "I give thanks to you, O Lord my God, with my whole heart, and I will glorify your name forever. For great is your steadfast love toward me." -Psalm 86:12-13

When we remember His love and faithfulness throughout our lives, our hearts can trust and rejoice in Him.

> "I will give thanks to the LORD with my whole heart; I will recount all of your wonderful deeds." -Psalm 9:1

This is what makes unbearable circumstances more bearable.

Our situations become more bearable when we set our mind on God and not on our circumstances. Thanking God despite our current reality is one of the best ways we can glorify Him. It's a significant way to be a witness for Christ. We show the outside world that truly our salvation is what brings us the greatest hope and deepest joy!

> "The one who offers thanksgiving as his sacrifice glorifies me; to one who orders his way rightly I will show the salvation of God!" -Psalm 50:23

It is when we are sincerely thankful that our hearts stop beating in complacency and become fervent for the Lord again.

> "I give you thanks, O Lord, with my whole heart; before the gods I sing your praise." -Psalm 138:1

> "Let the word of Christ dwell in you richly, teaching and admonishing one another in all wisdom, singing psalms and hymns and spiritual songs, with thankfulness in your hearts to God." -Colossians 3:16

> "My heart is steadfast, O God, my heart is steadfast! I will sing and make melody!" -Psalm 57:7

TAKE A MOMENT

1. Where have you become complacent in your faith?

2. In what situation can you be more intentionally thankful?

> *Heavenly Father, please forgive me for where I have become complacent in my relationship with You. I do not want to be lazy in my faith. Help me to grow in thankfulness for Your love, grace, faithfulness, and abundant blessings, so that my heart focuses on You and not my circumstances. May my thankful heart display to others that my salvation is what brings me hope and joy. Amen.*

DAY 17

DECEIVED HEART → TRUTH-FILLED HEART

Just because someone calls themselves a Christian doesn't mean they are one. This is true about "Christian" influencers, "Christian" writers, and "Christian" motivational speakers. Many influencers are posing to be of the Christian faith to teach and indoctrinate the body of Christ in completely unbiblical ways.

Romans 16:18 says,

> "For such persons do not serve our Lord Christ, but their own appetites, and by smooth talk and flattery they deceive the hearts of the naïve."

We must assess if our hearts are being deceived, even within the church itself.

Our hearts may be deceived by the health and wealth gospel that says if we live in obedience to Christ, we will have no sickness, and riches will pour into our lives. If we are sick, we must be living in sin. This is a false gospel. The Bible promises eternal riches to the faithful but suffering while on earth. We are promised persecution for following Christ and the Bible. We are not to hoard our wealth but to give it away for God's Kingdom and purposes.

Our deceiving hearts may try to look within ourselves to find a healing path. Popular teachers on the personality tool, "The Enneagram," are filling Christian bookshelves with their new age philosophies that our "true selves" have no sin. They teach that we are deceiving ourselves to believe we are sinful and separated from God. Yet, 1 John 1:8 says the exact opposite.

> "If we say we have no sin, we deceive ourselves, and the truth is not in us."

Their view is that Christ was incarnated into creation, and since we are part of creation, every person is "in Christ," and thus, the cross of Christ is unnecessary for our salvation.

Jesus says otherwise in John 14:6,

> "Jesus said to him, 'I am the way, and the truth, and the life. No one comes to the Father except through me.'"

The Enneagram personality types were given to a man named Claudio Naranjo through "automatic writing." Automatic writing is a form of spirit contact in which a person opens up a channel of communication from a supernatural source and allows the source to dictate the words. This tool was created through channeling spirits. It was then introduced into the New Age Movement, which was next accepted into the progressive Christian church and then permeated the evangelical church. This tool is far from Biblical, yet it is enticing young and old alike that are itching to learn "deeply hidden truths" about themselves so that they can be on the road to transformation. Even if the tool seems useful on the surface, the end never justifies the means. We cannot use what came from evil for our good, especially not to transform ourselves into better people. Only the Holy Spirit can do that.

Watch out for the persuasive talk of people, even in your church. We can be too highly trusting of spiritual leaders or "Christian" authors, and we can slowly become deceived. There is only ONE SOURCE for truth: God's perfect, unchanging, applicable Word.

John 17:17 says,

> "Sanctify them in the truth; your word is truth."

2 Timothy 3:16-17 says,

> "All scripture is breathed out by God and profitable for teaching, for reproof, for correction, and for training in righteousness, that the man of God may be complete, equipped for every good work."

Reading and applying the Bible is how we transform, not through outside, mystic tools handed down from other religions. We don't need psychics, tarot cards, palm readers, mediums, the Ouija board, fortune tellers, astrologers, or enneagrams to help us know ourselves and our futures. These modes of seeking truth will not set us free but will oppress us and distract us from the one true God and seeking truth in the Word only.

John 8:31-32 says,

> "So Jesus said to the Jews who had believed him, 'If you abide in my word, you are truly my disciples, and you will know the truth and the truth will set you free.'"

To have a truth-filled heart, we must be students of the Scriptures.

2 Timothy 2:15 says,

> "Do your best to present yourself to God as one approved, a worker who has no need to be ashamed, rightly handling the word of truth."

We must know correct theology about God, man, Christ, and salvation. We must test everything that intrigues us through the grid of the Word of God. Nothing is a substitute for the Bible when it comes to transforming our lives from the inside out.

"For if we go on sinning deliberately after receiving the knowledge of the truth, there no longer remains a sacrifice for sins, but a fearful expectation of judgment, and a fury of fire that will consume the adversaries." -Hebrews 10:26-27

"And I will ask the Father, and he will give you another Helper, to be with you forever, even the Spirit of truth, whom the world cannot receive, because it neither sees him nor knows him. You know him, for he dwells with you and will be in you." -John 14:16-17

"Deceit is in the heart of those who devise evil, but those who plan peace have joy." -Proverbs 12:20

"Every way of a man is right in his own eyes, but the Lord weights the heart." -Proverbs 21:2

"He feeds on ashes; a deluded heart has led him astray, and he cannot deliver himself or say, 'Is there not a lie in my right hand?'" -Isaiah 44:20

"They search out injustice, saying, 'We have accomplished a diligent search.' For the inward mind and heart of a man are deep." -Psalm 64:6

TAKE A MOMENT

1. Where might you have allowed outside wisdom to influence your faith and practices?

2. Why is it essential for us to evaluate everything according to Scripture?

> *Heavenly Father, I do not want to be deceived by persuasive and popular teachers or ideologies. Please help me to handle the Word of Truth rightly. Only Your Word can teach me the truth about God, myself, Christ, and salvation. Help me read Your Word more than any other teachings so that I can see counterfeit gospels when they are presented to me. Help me to know the truth so that Your truth will set me free. Amen.*

DAY 18

SORROWFUL HEART → GLAD HEART

Waves of grief come and go when there is a significant loss in our lives. Whether it's losing a career, our health, or a loved one, grief washes over us, consuming us with sorrow and anguish. Grief is how we internalize the experience of loss. It can feel as if we are drowning, unable to take a deep breath because the pain is so weighty on our hearts. The depth of emotional distress from fear, loneliness, despair, yearning, anxiety and emptiness creates a powerful vacuum that seems to suck the joy and hope out of our lives.

Mourning is how we outwardly express our grief. It is healthy to mourn. People in the Bible knew how to mourn well. When family members died, they would take the time to slow down, feel the pain, remember the person, and sit in it. They would allow their grief to be expressed physically by tearing their clothes. The loss of a person we love is real. It's deep. And it will happen to every one of us at some point in our lives.

Ecclesiastes 7:2-3 says that,

> "This is the end of all mankind, and the living will lay it to heart. Sorrow is better than laughter, for by sadness of face the heart is made glad."

How do we take a grieving, sorrowful heart and return to hope, joy, and gladness? Death is not the end. Death is a transition of life on earth to life in heaven. A loved one takes their last breath of polluted earthly air and takes their first breath of perfected celestial air. They are instantly in the presence of the Lord. They are immediately healed. They have no more illness, imperfection or pain. This perspective should bring our focus to the eternal life we have in Christ, not the temporal life we have on earth. We will see our loved ones again if they, too, had faith in Jesus as their Lord and Savior.

Jesus gave this message of hope to His disciples before He died in John 16:22,

> "So also you have sorrow now, but I will see you again, and your hearts will rejoice, and no one will take your joy from you."

We will never fully get over the loss of a loved one. A piece of our heart was taken, and we feel the absence of their presence. This is when we can invite The Presence to come and enter into our sorrowful hearts. David knew pain and loss well. He was alone and isolated. His heart was faint, and, at times, he thought he could not go on. In those dark moments, David called out to God.

He said in Psalm 61:2,

> "From the end of the earth I call to you when my heart is faint. Lead me to the rock that is higher than I."

He asked God to lead him out of the depths of despair. He asked God to give him the strength to go on.

He said in Psalm 73:26,

> "My flesh and my heart may fail, but God is the strength of my heart and my portion forever."

He trusted in God's love.

> "But I have trusted in your steadfast love; my heart shall rejoice in your salvation." -Psalm 13:5

The one thing He could rejoice in, no matter the grief, pain, or loss, was his eternal salvation. This was where he placed his hope. This is where he found his joy.

Our salvation is not just for eternity. Our salvation is now. God the Father wants to be with us in our grief. He wants to be our Great Comforter. David understood this. He knew that focusing on the Lord would enable him to grow in hope and gladness of heart.

> "I have set the Lord always before me; because he is at my right hand, I shall not be shaken. Therefore my heart is glad, and my whole being rejoices; my flesh also dwells secure. For you will not abandon my soul to Sheol, or let your holy one see corruption. You make known to me the path of life; in your presence there is fullness of joy; at your right hand are pleasures forevermore." -Psalm 16:8-11

God wants us to see He is walking before us, preparing us for the day ahead, maybe even the hour ahead. He is at our right hand, to give us the strength to take one step at a time. God has not abandoned us in our grief. He enters into it with us.

God understands devastating loss. He watched His only Son, Jesus, be beaten and murdered as a sinless, innocent man. God chose to place all of His wrath on His Son so that we won't ever have to experience His anger. He abandoned Jesus on the cross because Jesus took on the sins of the world so that we could receive His righteousness and be in the presence of God. God understands grief. God also understands that death is not the end. Jesus conquered death on the cross, and we, too, will conquer death one day and be in the presence of the Lord forever. For our hearts to become glad in times of sorrow, we must seek the presence of the Lord. It is there we will find peace, hope, and eventually gladness again.

"How long must I take counsel in my soul and have sorrow in my heart all the day? How long shall my enemy be exalted over me?" -Psalm 13:2

"My heart is in anguish within me; the terrors of death have fallen upon me." -Psalm 55:4

"O Lord, you hear the desire of the afflicted; you will strengthen their heart; you will incline your ear." -Psalm 10:17

"All the days of the afflicted are evil, but the cheerful of heart has a continual feast." -Proverbs 15:15

"Comfort your hearts and establish them in every good work and word." -2 Timothy 2:17

TAKE A MOMENT

1. Do you tend to run to God or away from God when you are grieving?

2. How can you practice inviting God into your seasons of mourning so that you can be encouraged by His presence?

> *Heavenly Father, You understand grief and loss. Thank You for offering me Your presence when I feel alone in my grief. Please come and comfort me with Your presence. Remind me of the joy of my salvation. I have hope that You will restore gladness in my life from the inside out. Amen.*

DAY 19

ANXIOUS HEART → PEACE-FILLED HEART

Anxiety affects 40 million Americans each year. Anxiety has risen due to the COVID pandemic, loss of jobs, political unrest, and social injustices. Fear, worry, and unease have increased in our current cultural climate. When unchecked, these feelings can affect our ability to function in everyday life. We might avoid certain situations or activities because they make us feel anxious. We have trouble concentrating on tasks or staying focused on the present. It becomes challenging to make decisions. We may have irrational fears about situations. Anxiety can lead to physical ailments like chest pains, heart palpitations, trouble breathing, frequent headaches, irritability, difficulty sleeping, and fatigue.

To stop anxiety, we must learn where it begins. Anxieties begin with our thoughts. When we continually meditate on something, we may start to feel unsafe, uncertain, and uncomfortable. We are thinking about things that we cannot have control over. This can lead us to down spiral in our thinking from one scenario to the next. Getting stuck in our thoughts and our feelings can consume us. Our hearts beat faster than they should. Blood pressure goes up. Our bodies are on high alert. We stop functioning in a calm, rational way. This can never be God's will for us.

God's will for us is to be strong in Him when things seem to unravel and are uncontrollable in life. He wants us to remember that He is in control, and He will save us from whatever situation we are experiencing.

The prophet Isaiah said in Isaiah 35:4,

> "Say to those who have an anxious heart, 'Be strong; fear not! Behold, your God will come with vengeance, with the recompense of God. He will come and save you.'"

God can save us from our anxiety. But where do we begin?

When anxiety arises, do we inwardly focus on it, or do we take action to overcome it? We must stop meditating on things that cause anxiety. But how do we stop thinking about those things? We must fill our minds with God, His Word, and what is true.

Isaiah 26:3 says,

> "You keep him in perfect peace whose mind is stayed on you, because he trusts in you."

Start reading the Bible. Reading aloud can help us hear God's words over our invading thoughts. The more we read the Word, the more we will trust God, and He will overwhelm our hearts with His peace. Let me say that again. We can be overwhelmed with peace! God can give us a supernatural peace that we cannot receive elsewhere.

As we meditate on God and His Word, we need to cry out to God to renew our minds and think about what He wants us to think.

Philippians 4:6-9 says,

> "Do not be anxious about anything, *(Can you believe He says anything?)* but in everything *(every single thought or concern)* by prayer and supplication with thanksgiving let your requests be made known to God. When we do this, look what happens. And the peace of God, which surpasses all understanding, will guard your hearts and your minds in Christ Jesus. He will guard our feelings and our thoughts! But what should we be thinking about? Finally, brothers, whatever is true, whatever is honorable, whatever is just, whatever is pure, whatever is lovely, whatever is commendable, if there is any excellence, if there

> is anything worthy of praise, think about these things. What you have learned and received and heard and seen in me—practice these things, and the God of peace will be with you."

This is a promise. When we intentionally practice controlling our thoughts by focusing on what is true, God's peace will be with us. Not only will God pour His peace over us, but He will also guard our hearts and minds against whatever we've been feeling or thinking that is destroying our peace!

This world will bring us twists and turns we aren't ready for emotionally. There are situations we can't solve or think about clearly. In those moments, we must stop trying to be God and allow God to take back control of our minds, of our emotions, and our lives.

In John 16:33, Jesus said,

> "I have said these things to you, that in me you may have peace. In the world you will have tribulation. But take heart; I have overcome the world."

In this fallen world, peace is not attainable unless we allow Christ to rule in our hearts. This means we are submitting our life to the ways of Christ found in the Bible.

Psalm 119:165 promises,

> "Great peace have those who love your law, nothing can make them stumble."

Internal peace comes when we know we are walking in His will by obeying and pleasing Him.

Peace comes when we have a trusting relationship with the Lord by intimately knowing Him. We trust He loves us, is with us, will guide and protect us, and has ultimate victory over all things. Trust dissolves our anxiety, giving us peace of mind and peace of emotions throughout the uncertain times in life. Let us take our thoughts captive, trust in God's promises and see how He will overwhelm us from the inside out with His peace. It truly surpasses all understanding!

> "Anxiety in a man's heart weights him down, but a good word makes him glad." -Proverbs 12:25
>
> "But watch yourselves lest your hearts be weighed down with dissipation and drunkenness and cares of this life, and that day come upon you suddenly like a trap." -Luke 21:34
>
> "Let not your heart be troubled. Believe in God; believe also in me." -John 14:1
>
> "The troubles of my heart are enlarged; bring me out of my distresses." -Psalm 25:17
>
> "And let the peace of Christ rule in your hearts, to which indeed you were called in one body. And be thankful."
> -Colossians 3:15

TAKE A MOMENT

1. What thoughts, when kept unchecked, create anxiety in your life?

2. How can you be more intentional to focus on God and His Word when anxiety creeps in to have better control over your thoughts?

> *Heavenly Father, please bless me and keep me. Make Your face shine upon me and be gracious to me. Take away my anxiety. Help me to focus on You. Help me to think about what is good, pure and lovely. Help me to trust You so that I have peace that passes all understanding in my heart. Amen.*

DAY 20

PRIDEFUL HEART → HUMBLE HEART

What sort of clothes we wear tells us a little about ourselves. Do we dress to impress? Do we dress for the job that needs to be done? Do we prefer basketball shorts or yoga pants over pinstriped suits and pencil skirts? No matter what we choose to wear or why, we put on something every day. Every day we take the time to decide how we will clothe ourselves.

The Bible tells us precisely what our wardrobe should consist of. It teaches us what we should faithfully wear each day, no matter who we are or what we do for a living. We are to put on humility.

1 Peter 5:5-6 says,

> "Clothe yourselves, all of you, with humility toward one another for God opposes the proud but gives grace to the humble. Humble yourselves, therefore, under the mighty hand of God so that at the proper time he may exalt you."

We are encouraged in the business world to dress for success. It doesn't matter the brand of our shoes or shirts that we wear if we don't have humility. If we chose to clothe ourselves with pride, focusing on what we've accomplished, we might receive brief admiration from others, but God will oppose us.

James 4:6 says,

> "God opposes the proud but gives grace to the humble."

Obadiah 1:3 says,

> "The pride of your heart has deceived you, you who live in the clefts of the rock, in your lofty dwelling, who say in your heart, 'Who will bring me down to the ground?'"

Satan is our quintessential example of a prideful heart and its ramifications. He is one of God's most physically beautiful angels when it comes to outward beauty. Yet, he chose to clothe his heart with pride. He wanted to take God's position in heaven, and because of that, God had him fall from heaven and no longer be one of his angels. Satan will receive the full wrath of God for his continual pride and rebellion at the end of time when he is thrown into the pit of hell.

Proverbs 16:5 warns us that,

> "Everyone who is arrogant in heart is an abomination to the Lord; be assured, he will not go unpunished."

Maybe we don't feel the ramifications of our pride, but Proverbs 16:18 says,

> "Pride goes before destruction, and a haughty spirit before a fall."

When we choose to live pridefully, we will experience consequences, if not in this life, then in the life to come.

Psalm 101:5 says,

> "Whoever slanders his neighbor secretly I will destroy. Whoever has a haughty look and an arrogant heart I will not endure."

We must assess if we have an arrogant heart because God will not be patient with our pride.

Here are some ways we can assess our hearts to see if we are walking in pride or humility: Proud people notice others' failures and are critical and judgmental. Humble people are overwhelmed by their sin and have mercy, compassion, and grace on others. Proud people look down on others. Humble people esteem others as better than themselves. Proud people appear self-sufficient and keep others at arm's length. Humble people recognize their need for others and are willing to be vulnerable. Proud people must be right. Humble people do not feel the need to be right because they don't assume they know everything. Proud people demand things and have expectations of others. Humble people surrender their rights for the sake of blessing others. Proud people protect their rights, time, possessions, and reputation. Humble people deny themselves and don't have their identity in those things. Proud people expect to be served. Humble people serve others. Proud people self-promote to advance themselves and to gain recognition and appreciation. Humble people look for opportunities to platform others to become successful and are thankful for whatever ways God uses them. Proud people feel confident in their knowledge and don't listen to others' advice. Humble people know they can grow in more wisdom and are teachable. Proud people are self-conscious and worry about their image. Humble people are not concerned with how others perceive them because their identity and confidence comes from the Lord.

1 Peter 3:8 says,

> "Finally, all of you, have unity of mind, sympathy, brotherly love, a tender heart, and a humble mind."

What we wear matters. Not on the outside, but the inside. The attitude of the heart dresses us for success in God's eyes. What if we care more about dressing our hearts in humility than what we wear on the outside? How might focusing on our character tell us more about our true selves than the clothes we wear? Let's focus on how we clothe ourselves internally each day, so we dress for God's plan and purpose for our lives.

"Haughty eyes and a proud heart, the lamp of the wicked, are sin." -Proverbs 21:4

"By your great wisdom in your trade you have increased your wealth, and your heart has become proud in your wealth." -Ezekiel 28:5

"Your heart was proud because of your beauty; you corrupted your wisdom for the sake of your splendor. I cast you to the ground; I exposed you before kings, to feast their eyes on you." -Ezekiel 28:17

"Before destruction a man's heart is haughty, but humility comes before honor." -Proverbs 18:12

"Then he said to me, 'Fear not, Daniel, for from the first day that you set your heart to understand and humble yourself before your God, your words have been heard, and I have come because of your words.'" -Daniel 10:12

"But Hezekiah humbled himself for the pride of his heart, both he and the inhabitants of Jerusalem, so that the wrath of the Lord did not come upon them in the days of Hezekiah." -2 Chronicles 32:26

TAKE A MOMENT

1. What prideful attitudes do you need to take off so that you can wear humility in your life?

2. How can wearing humility bring you success in your relationships and career?

> *Heavenly Father, please reveal to me where I have put on pride instead of humility. Help me to choose each morning to humble myself before You, remembering that I am saved by grace and desperately in need of Your mercy and forgiveness. Remind me that nothing I have accomplished has been by myself. May I decrease and may You increase in my life so that I can live out the character of humility. Amen.*

DAY 21

HOPELESS HEART → HOPEFUL HEART

When people become hopeless, death can seem more bearable than life. Life can hold such significant burdens. Destruction in our lives can seem unrepairable. Change doesn't appear possible. Light doesn't seem findable. Hope evaporates.

Proverbs 13:12 says,

> "Hope deferred makes the heart sick, but a desire fulfilled is a tree of life."

Hope links to our desires and expectations of what we think we need to be fulfilled. If our desires aren't met in the ways we expect, in the timing we assume is best, then we begin to lose hope. The more our focus is on wanting our desires fulfilled by our circumstances, rather than on God, the more vulnerable we are to experiencing hopelessness. Is our hope in having an intimate relationship with someone? Is our hope in getting a specific career or position? Is our hope that our friends and family are safe and secure without sickness, pain, or death? If our hope is in these things, then our hearts will be stuck in hopelessness and despair.

When we notice we are feeling hopeless due to a situation in our lives, our first step is to pray and ask God to help us not lose heart.

Jesus said this in Luke 18:1,

> "And he told them a parable to the effect that they ought always to pray and not lose heart."

God refocuses us to have hope about our eternal future with Him and not hope for the temporal things this world promises will satisfy us.

Ephesians 1:18 says,

> "Having the eyes of your hearts enlightened, that you may know what is the hope to which he has called you, what are the riches of his glorious inheritance in the saints."

Hope can only come from God.

Psalm 62:5 says,

> "For God alone, O my soul, wait in silence, for my hope is from him."

God's plan is to give us hope.

Jeremiah 29:11-13 says,

> "For I know the plans I have for you, declares the LORD, plans for welfare and not for evil, to give you a future and a hope. Then you will call upon me and come and pray to me, and I will hear you. You will seek me and find me, when you seek me with all your heart."

We find hope when our greatest desire shifts from earthly longings to longing to experience Him in His Word.

Psalms 130:5 says,

> "I wait for the LORD, my soul waits, and in his word, I hope."

When we realize our hope can only come from God, we can grasp that our hope can only be in God.

Psalm 43:5 says,

> "Why are you cast down, O my soul, and why are you in turmoil within me? Hope in God; for I shall again praise him, my salvation and my God."

Our greatest hope is in His love. In God's love, He created us and has a purpose for our lives. By Jesus' love, He willingly died a brutal death to save us from our sins and eternal separation from Him. It is because of God's love that He placed the Holy Spirit inside of us to comfort us, conform us to His image, and communicate with us how to live this life moment by moment. Grasping God's love for us is what gives us hope, no matter what desires are unmet in our hearts.

Psalm 33:18-22 says,

> "Behold, the eye of the LORD is on those who fear him, on those who hope in his steadfast love, that he may deliver their soul from death and keep them alive in famine.
> Our soul waits for the LORD; he is our help and our shield. For our heart is glad in him, because we trust in his holy name. Let your steadfast love, O LORD, be upon us, even as we hope in you."

Lamentations 3:17-25 shows us that when we feel hopeless, we must remember God's love never ceases.

> "My soul is bereft of peace; I have forgotten what happiness is; so, I say, 'My endurance has perished; so, has my hope from the LORD.' Remember my affliction and my wanderings, the wormwood and the gall! My soul continually remembers it and is bowed down within me. But this I call to mind, and therefore I have hope: The steadfast love of the LORD never ceases; his mercies never come to an end; they are new every morning; great is your faithfulness. 'The LORD is my portion,' says my soul, 'therefore I will hope in him.' The LORD is good to those who wait for him, to the soul who seeks him."

It is the role of the Holy Spirit to pour God's love in our hearts. If we feel hopeless, we can cry out to the Spirit to overwhelm us with God's love.

Romans 5:3-5 says,

> "Not only that, but we rejoice in our sufferings, knowing that suffering produces endurance, and endurance produces character, and character produces hope, and hope does not put us to shame, because God's love has been poured into our hearts through the Holy Spirit who has been given to us."

We will have hope, we will have endurance, even in great suffering, when we grasp how incredibly loved we are by God. He died specifically for you. There is no greater love. There is no better place to put your hope than in Him. Rest in His love, and He will give you hope from the inside out.

> "If you prepare your heart, you will stretch out your hands toward him. If iniquity is in your hand, put it far away, and let not injustice dwell in your tents. Surely then you will lift up your face without blemish; you will be secure and will not fear. You will forget your misery; you will remember it as waters that have passed away. And your life will be brighter than the noonday; its darkness will be like the morning. And you will feel secure, because there is hope; you will look around and take your rest in security."
> -Job 11:13-18

> "For in this hope we were saved. Now hope that is seen is not hope. For who hopes for what he sees? But if we hope for what we do not see, we wait for it with patience."
> -Romans 8:24-25

"Rejoice in hope, be patient in tribulation, be constant in prayer." -Romans 12:12

TAKE A MOMENT

1. Where has your hope been misplaced onto things of this life rather than on God?

2. How can experiencing God's love lead you to maintain hope in your current circumstances?

> *Heavenly Father, I want to pray Romans 15:13 into my life. "May the God of hope fill me with all joy and peace in believing, so that by the power of the Holy Spirit I may abound in hope." I also pray 2 Thessalonians 2:16-17 into my life. "Now may our Lord Jesus Christ himself, and God our Father, who loved us and gave us eternal comfort and good hope through grace, comfort my heart and establish me in every good work and word." Help me to experience Your love in such a way that I abound in hope. Amen.*

DAY 22
SELFISH HEART → GENEROUS HEART

When my son was seven years old we give him a quarter for every book he read. He saved $125 intending to get an expensive Lego set. Christmas time came around, and I put a Compassion International magazine in front of him. I asked him what he wanted to buy with his money to bless those in need. He read that he could buy ten Bibles for $100. He said he wanted to do that. I tried to talk him down. "Son, do you really want to spend most of your money on Bibles, and not just buy one or two? You won't have enough for a Lego set." *(Forget the fact that I'm a missionary, and the reason I showed him the magazine was that I wanted him to give generously!)* He looked at me with resolve and said, "Yes, mom. I want ten kids to have Bibles so that they can learn about Jesus." Now, that is a generous heart with an eternal mindset. I was convicted that day that I actually could have hindered him from joyfully giving.

2 Corinthians 9:7 says,

> "Each one must give as he has decided in his heart, not reluctantly or under compulsion, for God loves a cheerful giver."

Who am I to say what is too much to give? Especially when it comes to giving to the poor and giving toward spiritual things.

We might be hesitant to give money directly to the poor, not trusting what they will do with it. If that's the case, we can provide non-monetary gifts like food, clothing, and even friendship. The first church in Acts saw that lives changed when they were generous.

Acts 2:46-47 says,

> "And day by day, attending the temple together and breaking bread in their homes, they received their food with glad and generous hearts, praising God and having favor

> with all people. And the Lord added to their number daily those who were being saved."

I never thought I could experience this Acts passage, but I did in none-other-than Berkeley, California. I was going on a mission trip for the summer, and my apartment would be vacant. I knew of a homeless man named Ken, who attended our church and "lived" in the infamous "People's Park" downtown. One day, I felt that God wanted me to offer him my apartment for the summer, free of cost so that he can get back on his feet and get a job. *(Many homeless can't get jobs because they don't have a permanent address.)*

1 John 3:17 came to my mind,

> "But if anyone has the world's goods and sees his brother in need, yet closes his heart against him, how does God's love abide in him?"

That very day I offered him my apartment, and he gladly accepted it!

That simple gift of letting him stay in my place gave him the address he needed to get a job and find his own apartment by the end of the summer. But that's not all. He started to take what he learned on Sunday mornings at church and teach it to his friends at the park in the afternoon. He'd bring PB&J sandwiches, sit down, and preach. Many came to Christ that summer, and he started a church in the park for the homeless. When I came back, he told me that he felt called to be a missionary in Africa! Wow! I had no clue offering my apartment *(which many people thought was unwise for me to do)* would bear so much spiritual fruit!

When our hearts are generous, lives are changed, people are saved. Are we giving generously to eternal things? Or are we only investing and spending toward the temporal? Are we hoarding our money for things that will rust, tear, and fade away? Or are we investing in the lives of others who will spread the gospel?

James 3:14-16 says,

> "But if you have bitter jealousy and selfish ambition in your hearts, do not boast and be false to the truth. This is not the wisdom that comes down from above, but is earthly, unspiritual, demonic. For where jealousy and selfish ambition exist, there will be disorder and every vile practice."

Have you ever considered that not giving generously to those in need is not only selfish but is part of Satan's plan to derail us from receiving God's blessings in our lives?

The Apostle Paul says in Acts 20:35,

> "In all things I have shown you that by working hard in this way we must help the weak and remember the words of the Lord Jesus, how he himself said, 'It is more blessed to give than to receive.'"

God might ask us to be generous with our time, talents, or treasure. A generous heart comes when we start to give. Then we trust God and give more. My husband and I have learned that we can't out-give God. When God asks us to give, and we trust Him to do so, He blesses us all the more! Let us begin to have generous hearts by giving cheerfully and see what God will do around us!

> "And they come to you as people come, and they sit before you as my people, and they hear what you say but they will not do it; for with lustful talk in their mouths they act; their heart is set on their gain." -Ezekiel 33:31

> "Take from among you a contribution to the Lord. Whoever is of a generous heart, let him bring the Lord's contribution: gold, silver and bronze." -Exodus 35:5

"All the men and women, the people of Israel, whose heart moved them to bring anything for the work that the Lord had commanded by Moses to be done brought it as a freewill offering to the Lord." -Exodus 35:29

"The wicked borrows but does not pay back, but the righteous is generous and gives." -Psalms 37:21

"Whoever oppresses a poor man insults his Maker, but he who is generous to the needy honors him." -Proverbs 14:31

"Whoever is generous to the poor lends to the LORD, and he will repay him for his deed." -Proverbs 19:17

"Do nothing from selfish ambition or conceit, but in humility count others more significant than yourselves."
-Philippians 2:3

"They are to do good, to be rich in good works, to be generous and ready to share, thus storing up treasure for themselves as a good foundation for the future, so that they may take hold of that which is truly life." -1 Timothy 6:18-19

TAKE A MOMENT

1. Where have you been selfish with your time, talents, or treasure?

2. Where might God be nudging you to be more generous?

> *Heavenly Father, please show me where I am selfish with my time, talents, and treasure. "Incline my heart to your testimonies, and not to selfish gain" (Psalm 119:36)! Help me to become more generous and hold these things with open hands. I trust that You will bless me as I freely give to others. Amen.*

DAY 23

OVERLY-SENSITIVE HEART → GRACE-FILLED HEART

Some of us may be more sensitive to what people say and do around us. We may get easily offended and take things personally that we shouldn't. Someone makes a joke about our mother, and we're swinging at them to defend her name. People offend us knowingly and unknowingly. Even if people are intentionally trying to push our buttons, we choose how to respond. An overly sensitive heart tends to react impulsively rather than respond in a Godly manner. If our hearts remain overly sensitive, we will isolate ourselves from further pain or fight back with equally offensive words. Both responses will destroy relationships. We will be a ticking time bomb ready to fight about anything or a fragile individual who could break by a reckless comment. Both reactions lead to people not wanting to engage with us in deep conversations due to fear of how we might respond. We become unsafe people. People's words should not have this much power over us and how we respond.

It helps to remember that everyone is a sinner around us, including ourselves. We have offended others. We have been rude. We have been disrespectful. We have been judgmental. When we remember that we are not righteous either, we can take less offense to what others say to us in the heat of the moment.

Ecclesiastes 7:20-22 says,

> "Surely there is not a righteous man on earth who does good and never sins. Do not take to heart all the things that people say, lest you hear your servant cursing you. Your heart knows that many times you have cursed others."

Maybe our hearts aren't overly sensitive to others but, instead, are overly critical. People can quickly irritate us, and we act in frustration toward them. This is called vexation.

Ecclesiastes 11:10 tells us that we create inner turmoil when we don't remove vexation from our hearts.

> "Remove vexation from your heart, and put away pain from your body, or youth and the dawn of life are vanity."

Sometimes, what we negatively think about others comes out in our speech toward them.

Ephesians 4:29 command us to,

> "Let no corrupting talk come out of your mouths, but only such as is good for building up, as fits the occasion, that it may give grace to those who hear."

We must intentionally give grace with our words even if someone is not providing grace with theirs. Grace is giving someone something they may not deserve. We are to give grace to the person who offends us and the person who annoys us.

How can we find the ability to be grace-filled people? We begin by going to the grace-filled throne in prayer. It is there we will grasp our need for God's grace in such a way we will be able to give grace freely to others.

Hebrews 4:16 says,

> "Let us then with confidence draw near to the throne of grace, that we may receive mercy and find grace to help in time of need."

God gives us His grace so that we can give our grace to others.

This is one of the most explicit ways we can live out the gospel to others. The gospel is about God offering us His grace so that we can be reconciled to Him and have a relationship. When we offer our grace to others, they experience God's grace in action.

The Apostle Paul urges us to do this in 2 Corinthians 8:7.

> "But as you excel in everything—in faith, in speech, in knowledge, in all earnestness, and in our love for you—see that you excel in this act of grace also."

Paul knew that when we excel in offering grace to others, we are acting counter-culturally than how the world behaves. This is one of our greatest testimonies that God changes our hearts.

We can give grace to those who hurt and offend us because we don't expect that they can heal the hurt they have caused. Only God can heal us from the offenses of others.

1 Peter 5:10 says,

> "And after you have suffered a little while, the God of all grace, who has called you to his eternal glory in Christ, will himself restore, confirm, strengthen, and establish you."

It is God who restores us when we are offended. God will strengthen us to brush it off and move forward with others by extending grace. This grace-filled heart will not only change us from the inside out but significantly impact the lives around us!

> "For it is all for your sake, so that as grace extends to more and more people it may increase thanksgiving, to the glory of God." -2 Corinthians 4:15

> "And God is able to make all grace abound to you, so that having all sufficiency in all things at all times, you may abound in every good work." -2 Corinthians 9:8

"Therefore lift your drooping hands and strengthen your weak knees, and make straight paths for your feet, so that what is lame may not be put out of joint but rather be healed. Strive for peace with everyone, and for the holiness without which no one will see the Lord. See to it that no one fails to obtain the grace of God; that no "root of bitterness" springs up and causes trouble, and by it many become defiled." -Hebrews 12:12-15

TAKE A MOMENT

1. How has being overly sensitive affected you and those around you?

2. What is the benefit to choosing to excel at giving grace instead of staying critical of others?

> *Heavenly Father, I enter Your throne room of grace, asking You to give me the strength to give grace to those who have offended me or annoyed me. Remind me of the grace You have given me that I do not deserve. Remind me that giving grace to others will enable me to live out the gospel and see lives change. Please restore relationships where I have been overly sensitive or critical. Help me admit where I have wronged others and ask for their forgiveness. Amen.*

DAY 24

HATEFUL HEART → LOVING HEART

In our upside-down world, sometimes hating others seems like a righteous attitude. The world says it is appropriate to hate murderers, adulterers, rapists, slanderers, child abusers, bigots and racists. Even as we read that list and think of all the evil, the destruction, and even the hate the exudes from them, God says we are not to hate them. Just because someone has sinned and grievously harmed others, we are not given the green light to hate them for it.

Leviticus 19:17 says,

> "You shall not hate your brother in your heart, but you shall reason frankly with your neighbor, lest you incur sin because of him."

When we hate others, we fall into our own sin in our hearts.

God completely abhors sin. Sin is what ignites the wrath of God toward the unjust and immoral. They will receive the full punishment for their actions when confronted by Jesus at the Judgement Seat of Christ. No sin will go unpunished, and they will experience the wrath of God for all eternity. But for now, earth is a moment in time where God's love and grace are offered even to the worst of sinners. Jesus died for all people because all people are made in God's image. It is up to them if they cry out to the Lord for forgiveness and repent of their sins. If they do, they will receive the grace of God at the Great White Throne of Judgement and be welcomed into His presence. This does not mean they won't receive consequences on earth. Justice is right and appropriate, but hating them is not.

Proverbs 24:17 says,

> "Do not rejoice when your enemy falls, and let not your heart be glad when he stumbles."

We need to see even the worst of sinners as completely lost and in need of God's love, grace and forgiveness. Only then will they be transformed and stop their evil acts toward others.

We are challenged to have a loving heart toward others, hoping that they will see Christ in us and want to turn to Him for mercy.

1 Peter 4:8 says,

> "Above all, keep loving one another earnestly, since love covers a multitude of sins."

This does not mean we cover up or defend the sin of another. It means we do not damn them on this side of eternity because our love and forgiveness just might be what saves them.

Jesus says in Matthew 5:43-45,

> "You have heard that it was said, 'You shall love your neighbor and hate your enemy.' But I say to you, 'Love your enemies and pray for those who persecute you, so that you may be sons of your Father who is in heaven.'"

Jesus teaches us to do something that might seem downright impossible to do. We are to pray for someone who is intentionally against us. Jesus asks us to do this because then we truly have His heart for the lost. He died even for those who abandoned Him in His greatest time of need. He died for those who condemned Him to the cross. He died for those who whipped His back, spat on His face, and pounded nails in His hands. Jesus lived out what He is asking us to do: love our enemies.

It might seem impossible to love our enemies enough to care about their eternal destiny. Our perspective needs to change and see that loving our enemies is one of the greatest gifts we can give to God. It is a form of worship.

Mark 12:33 says,

> "And to love him with all the heart and with all the understanding and with all the strength, and to love one's neighbor as oneself, is much more than all whole burnt offerings and sacrifices."

This is about our trust in God's character. He is entirely merciful and just, even toward our enemies. Our role is to love so that lost people might come to repentance. God's role is to pursue the sinner, offer His grace, and give it to those who repent. God's part is also to judge the unrepentant and condemn them. Our hearts must relinquish holding onto hate if we want to have the loving heart God asks us to have toward others.

When I served in East Asia, I was sexually assaulted on a bus. The man had his hands all over me, touching me in inappropriate ways. Everyone on the bus seemed to look away, allowing it to happen. I froze in fear. I couldn't defend myself. I let it happen.

When I got home, I fell in the house's doorframe and cried. I felt violated and abandoned. I listen to worship music to get my mind on the Lord. That's when I sensed Him speaking to me. "Holly, will you forgive this man for what he did to you? He did it in public, which not only shames him but all the people around him in his culture. He is so lost. He didn't know what he was doing." I chose in my heart to forgive.

Then God asked, "Holly, will you pray for this man's salvation? If he believes in me, he will stop sexually assaulting women and be healed from sexual addiction." I chose in my heart to pray for his salvation.

But then, the Lord asked me the most challenging question of all, "Holly, can you thank Me that this happened to you and not some other woman on the bus? You see, his actions may have so damaged another woman, she would down-spiral into letting men continue to abuse her, and she'd be enslaved by her insecurities. You have me. You will heal. I am with you. I allowed this to happen to you because I know you are already Mine, and we can walk through this together."

Whew! It took all of me to say, "Thank you, Lord, for allowing this to happen to me instead of others." But when I did, I was free. There was no hate left in my heart, which is when I was able to begin healing.

When we feel hate consuming us, it is time for us to sit at the foot of the cross. Remember, we too deserve the wrath of God, and yet, He's given us His grace and love. We are no better than our enemies. We are all sinners equally in need of a Savior. This realization will give us the courage to surrender our hate and pursue loving our enemies from the inside out.

> "But I say to you who hear, love your enemies, do good to those who hate you, bless those who curse you, pray for those who abuse you." -Luke 6:27-28
>
> "By this all people will know that you are my disciples, if you have love for one another." -John 13: 35
> "This is my commandment, that you love one another as I have loved you." -John 15:12
>
> "Having purified your souls by your obedience to the truth for a sincere brotherly love, love one another earnestly from a pure heart." -1 Peter 1:22

“Beloved, let us love one another, for love is from God, and whoever loves has been born of God and knows God.”
-1 John 4:7

“with all humility and gentleness, with patience, bearing with one another in love.” -Ephesians 4:2

TAKE A MOMENT

1. Who have you thought it was ok to hate but now know it's not?

2. Who is God bringing to mind that you need to forgive, pray for, and love better?

> *Heavenly Father, change my heart. Some people are very hard to forgive and love in my life. It is hard to understand why I am to love evil people. Help me have Your heart and desire for them to know You so that they can change and stop hurting others. Help me to worship You with my whole heart by loving people who hate me. Amen.*

DAY 25

ANGRY HEART → FORGIVING HEART

Psychologists explain that anger is considered a secondary emotion. Usually, under the thick exterior of anger is fear or sadness. Fear can be from anxiety or worry. Sadness can stem from loss, disappointment, or discouragement. These underlying feelings may be uncomfortable and cause us to not feel in control. To avoid these emotions, we can subconsciously transfer them into anger. Anger gives us the illusion that we are in control and have power, when, in reality, under the surface, we feel uncertain and vulnerable. Understanding where the anger stems from helps us deal with it healthily so that we aren't trapped in an emotion that will destroy us and those around us.

The wisest man who ever lived, King Solomon, says in Ecclesiastes 7:9,

> "Be not quick in your spirit to become angry, for anger lodges in the heart of fools."

The more we meditate on what angers us, the angrier we become.

Hosea 7:6 says,

> "For with hearts like an oven they approach their intrigue; all night their anger smolders; in the morning it blazes like a flaming fire."

Anger can become addicting. We feel powerful. Unfortunately, the power of anger creates an unsafe environment. This causes people to avoid us and destroys our chance for deep, intimate community where we can be fully known and loved.

Not all anger is a sin. God gets angry and is without sin. It is how we react when we are angry that can be sinful.

Psalm 4:4 says,

> "Be angry, and do not sin; ponder in your own hearts on your beds, and be silent."

We are to consider how to respond Biblically to an offense and remain silent until we can respond without anger.

Psalm 37:8 says,

> "Refrain from anger, and forsake wrath! Fret not yourself; it tends only to evil."

When we continue to mull over an offense and fret about it, we will, at some moment, explode with words that are not wise or helpful.

Psalm 39:3 says,

> "My heart became hot within me. As I mused, the fire burned; then I spoke with my tongue."

Our anger usually stirs up more conflict and creates another layer of sin to work through.

Proverbs 29:22 says,

> "A man of wrath stirs up strife, and one given to anger causes much transgression."

We are to be slow in getting angry.

Proverbs 14:29 says,

> "Whoever is slow to anger has great understanding, but he who has a hasty temper exalts folly."

James 1:19-20 gives us this advice,

> "Know this, my beloved brothers: let every person be quick to hear, slow to speak, slow to anger; for the anger of man does not produce the righteousness of God."

It is unwise, unproductive, and unrighteous to respond in anger.

Anger is like a fire, and the only thing that can put it out is a heart of forgiveness.

Ephesians 4:31-32 says,

> "Let all bitterness and wrath and anger and clamor and slander be put away from you, along with all malice. Be kind to one another, tenderhearted, forgiving one another, as God in Christ forgave you."

The Apostle Paul says to put bitterness, wrath, and anger far away from us. The moment we are angry, we need to choose what to do with it. Will we stew over it? Will we get others angry along with us through slander and gossip? Paul says our response to others should not be to react in anger or slander but to be kind and forgive..

We are again being called out to live differently than the world. The world wants us to be angry and act wrathfully toward others when injustice happens. Though righteous anger is Biblical, this does not give us the license to act out angrily to demand justice. What if the best way to get justice is to begin with kindness? What if we forgave those who were unjust?

Luke 6:37 says,

> "Judge not, and you will not be judged; condemn not, and you will not be condemned; forgive, and you will be forgiven."

God is the judge, and His wrath will fall on the unrighteous.

The Bible commands us to forgive.

Colossians 3:13 says,

> "Bearing with one another and, if one has a complaint against another, forgiving each other; as the Lord has forgiven you, so you also must forgive."

We are asked to forgive anyone for anything. That seems practically impossible. Forgiveness is a beautiful gift to receive, but it's challenging to give. Some of us have been grievously harmed by others, which seems like an impossible expectation Jesus is placing on us. CS Lewis says, "To be a Christian means to forgive the inexcusable because God has forgiven the inexcusable in us." God has forgiven everything we have done, no matter the gravity of the offense. He is calling us to do the same. No ifs, ands, or buts about it!

Instead of mulling over the situation and simmering in our anger, we are called to pray when we are angry.

Mark 11:25 says,

> "And whenever you stand praying, forgive, if you have anything against anyone, so that your Father also who is in heaven may forgive you your trespasses."

Jesus expects us to forgive if we desire the Father to forgive us. When we refuse to forgive, we give Satan an advantage in our lives to control our emotions and responses. He wants us to stay in our anger because he knows it will lead to bitterness, and bitterness leads to death.

Forgiveness is an attitude of letting go of resentment and our right to get even. We leave the ramifications to God to handle. We cannot stay in our anger and hope for a good outcome in any relationship. No relationship can move forward to heal without forgiveness being extended first. The ultimate goal in granting forgiveness is to bring glory and honor to God. Forgiveness is an opportunity to be part of something eternal, to shower our gratitude on the One who forgave us for everything. It's an offering, a sacrifice, a love gift to God for Him and Him alone. It is also a credible way to show the world that the gospel is real. When we extend forgiveness to others, it is a vivid testimony of God working in our lives and how much we trust Him. When we let go of our anger and forgive, we are changed from the inside out, and healing can begin.

> "The heart knows its own bitterness, and no stranger shares its joy." -Proverbs 14:10
>
> "A hot-tempered man stirs up strife, but he who is slow to anger quiets contention." -Proverbs 15:18
>
> "The godless in heart cherish anger; they do not cry for help when he binds them." -Job 36:13
>
> "For if you forgive others their trespasses, your heavenly Father will also forgive you, but if you do not forgive others their trespasses, neither will your Father forgive your trespasses." -Matthew 6:14-15

TAKE A MOMENT

1. Whom have you been angry with that you need to pray for?

2. Who do you need to forgive in your heart so that you can experience God's grace and forgiveness in your own life?

> *Heavenly Father, help me better understand what I feel when I get angry. Help me to go to You with my anger so that I do not react in wrath but respond in love, kindness, and forgiveness. Thank You for being a righteous judge who will handle the unjust in Your timing. Help me to show the world that the gospel is real by choosing, by faith, to forgive others. Amen.*

DAY 26

EVIL HEART → RIGHTEOUS HEART

When we think of people with evil hearts, we might think of Adolf Hitler and Saddam Hussein or even movie characters like Darth Vader or Maleficent. They knew they were evil and reveled in it. We, though, might have no clue that evil is hiding in our hearts and righteousness is far from us.

Hebrews 3:12-13 warns us,

> "Take care, brothers, lest there be in any of you an evil, unbelieving heart, leading you to fall away from the living God. But exhort one another every day, as long as it is called "today," that none of you may be hardened by the deceitfulness of sin."

We know that some things are blatantly evil, like genocide and child prostitution. But what if we are deceived into thinking some things aren't as evil as God says they are? What if evil is lodged in our hearts and we don't know it?

Romans 3:10 reminds us that,

> "None is righteous, no, not one."

Jesus knew this better than anyone. When he saw people who thought they were righteous, He said to them,

> "You brood of vipers! How can you speak good, when you are evil? For out of the abundance of the heart the mouth speaks." -Matthew 12:34

Evil can be undetected because it doesn't always seem to have consequences. We go unchecked in what we say and do.

> "Because the sentence against an evil deed is not executed speedily, the heart of the children of man is fully set to do evil." -Ecclesiastes 8:11

Evil in our hearts usually manifests in what we say. Our tongue can either be used to bless or curse others. Unfortunately, our tongues are one of the most challenging areas to have under control.

James 3:8-10 says,

> "No human being can tame the tongue. It is a restless evil, full of deadly poison. With it we bless our Lord and Father, and with it we curse people who are made in the likeness of God. From the same mouth come blessing and cursing. My brothers, these things ought not to be so."

Everyone is made in the image of God, and thus, even if someone says or does something evil toward us, we are to not respond in kind. Wanting to "get even" is part of having an evil heart.

1 Peter 3:9-12 says,

> "Do not repay evil for evil or reviling for reviling, but on the contrary, bless, for to this you were called, that you may obtain a blessing. For whoever desires to love life and see good days, let him keep his tongue from evil and his lips from speaking deceit; let him turn away from evil and do good; let him seek peace and pursue it. For the eyes of the Lord are on the righteous, and his ears are open to their prayer. But the face of the Lord is against those who do evil."

If we want to pursue a righteous heart, we must ponder how to answer without malicious intent, without hatred, slander, or spite.

Proverbs 15:28 says,

> "The heart of the righteous ponders how to answer, but the mouth of the wicked pours out evil things."

Psalm 37:30 says,

> "The mouth of the righteous utters wisdom, and his tongue speaks justice."

We know our heart is righteous when we can say,

> "All the words of my mouth are righteous; there is nothing twisted or crooked in them." -Proverbs 8:8

We can also observe what sort of fruit is being produced by the words we speak to others.

Luke 6:45 says,

> "The good person out of the good treasure of his heart produces good, and the evil person out of his evil treasure produces evil, for out of the abundance of the heart his mouth speaks."

The frustrating thing is that even when we want to say the right things, so often, our "good intentions" go to the wayside, and we slip up. The Apostle Paul understood this all too well.

He says in Romans 7:18-19,

> "For I know that nothing good dwells in me, that is, in my flesh. For I have the desire to do what is right, but not the ability to carry it out. For I do not do the good I want, but the evil I do not want is what I keep on doing."

This is a very defeating place to be, especially when we know how our words harm others.

Proverbs 12:13 says,

> "An evil man is ensnared by the transgression of his lips, but the righteous escapes from trouble."

Psalm 34:13 says,

> "Keep your tongue from evil and your lips from speaking deceit."

How can we get out of the snares our words have entangled us in? How can we keep our tongues from evil? We can escape by inviting the Holy Spirit to empower us to control our tongues. He alone is the solution for taming our tongue so that we bless instead of curse. For many Christ-followers, the Holy Spirit is like this gift they've been given that stays wrapped.

Luke 11:13 says that God wants to freely give us the Holy Spirit so that we can live a righteous life.

> "If you then, who are evil, know how to give good gifts to your children, how much more will the heavenly Father give the Holy Spirit to those who ask him!"

If we want to purge the evil from our hearts and live a righteous life, we need to invite the Holy Spirit to change our hearts. Only with His help can we be transformed from the inside out!

> "Do not devise evil in your hearts against one another, and love no false oath, for all these things I hate, declares the Lord." -Zechariah 8:17

"A perverse heart shall be far from me; I will know nothing of evil." -Psalm 101:4

"Repay no one evil for evil, but give thought to do what is honorable in the sight of all. If possible, so far as it depends on you, live peaceably with all. Beloved, never avenge yourselves, but leave it to the wrath of God, for it is written, "Vengeance is mine, I will repay, says the Lord." To the contrary, "if your enemy is hungry, feed him; if he is thirsty, give him something to drink; for by so doing you will heap burning coals on his head." Do not be overcome by evil, but overcome evil with good. -Romans 12:17-21

"Speak evil of no one, to avoid quarreling, to be gentle, and to show perfect courtesy toward all people." -Titus 3:2

"Who plan evil things in their heart and stir up wars continually. They make their tongue sharp as a serpent's, and under their lips is the venom of asps." -Psalm 140:2-3

"Deceit is in the heart of those who devise evil, but those who plan peace have joy." -Proverbs 12:20

"A worthless man plots evil, and his speech is like a scorching fire." -Proverbs 16:27

"The righteous hates falsehood, but the wicked brings shame and disgrace." -Proverbs 13:5

TAKE A MOMENT

1. What words have you said that are unrighteous toward others?

2. With whom do you need to let go of "getting even" and try to be a blessing instead?

> *Heavenly Father, please empower me with the Holy Spirit to overcome the evil that is on my tongue and bless others instead. It is hard not to get even, but I want to have Your righteous heart toward others. May the Holy Spirit give me the strength to speak words that bring life. Amen.*

DAY 27

FEARFUL HEART → COURAGEOUS HEART

Conspiracy theories seem to be multiplying as people try to make sense of our world. What is really going on behind the scenes? Be it in the government, the health industry, the stock market, or the elite in Hollywood, conspiracy theories are becoming front-page news. When we don't know what is happening or what will happen in the future, we can become fearful.

Isaiah 8:12 says,

> "Do not call conspiracy all that this people calls conspiracy, and do not fear what they fear, nor be in dread."

How are we not to live in fear when the world around us seems to be so untrustworthy? We don't know who to trust or what is true anymore.

Fear controls some of us. We fear for our safety or our children's safety. We fear what people may think of us. We are afraid to go where God is asking us to go or do what God is asking us to do because the risk seems too great. The Israelites were also controlled by fear. When they arrived at the edge of the Promised Land and spied out the people who lived there, they felt like the inhabitants were too strong and powerful to conquer. With their eyes, the cities seemed too great to overcome.

Here's what they said in Deuteronomy 1:28-33,

> "Where are we going up? Our brothers have made our hearts melt, saying, "The people are greater and taller than we. The cities are great and fortified up to heaven. And besides, we have seen the sons of the Anakim there.'"

Moses reminded them to be courageous because God is on their side.

> "Then I said to you, 'Do not be in dread or afraid of them. The LORD your God who goes before you will himself fight for you, just as he did for you in Egypt before your eyes, and in the wilderness, where you have seen how the LORD your God carried you, as a man carries his son, all the way that you went until you came to this place.' Yet in spite of this word you did not believe the LORD your God, who went before you in the way to seek you out a place to pitch your tents, in fire by night and in the cloud by day, to show you by what way you should go."

The Israelites only trusted what they could see, not what God promised them. They allowed their fear of men to stop them from gaining their inheritance.

When we misplace our trust, fear will arise. We aren't to put our trust in people's opinions. We aren't to put our trust in money. Instead, we are to put our trust in God. It is God who goes before us. He fights for us. He has a plan. He will have the final victory. Do our hearts trust God when there are significant obstacles in front of us? Are our hearts full of fear or full of faith? Do we shy away from what God is asking us to do? Do we take a stand against injustice? Do we share the gospel? These steps of faith require us to have hearts of courage.

God says to Joshua in Joshua 1:9,

> "Have I not commanded you? Be strong and courageous. Do not be frightened, and do not be dismayed, for the LORD your God is with you wherever you go."

God is encouraging Joshua to move forward to fight and retrieve the Promised Land. He had to lead in faith and courage while the Israelites felt fearful. Our calling is to be strong in our faith and courageous also. Children are growing up in the most anxious, fearful generation ever. They need us to bravely step up, moving forward in faith believing that God is with us, God goes before us, and God will have His plans accomplished in the end.

2 Samuel 10:12-13 says,

> "'Be of good courage, and let us be courageous for our people, and for the cities of our God, and may the LORD do what seems good to him.' So Joab and the people who were with him drew near to battle against the Syrians, and they fled before him."

We need to be courageous to fight the battles that will save the next generation: battles against sexual immorality, battles between our secular culture, and battles for the souls of the people around us.

When God invites us to enter into His work and fight the good fight, He will be with us.

In 1 Chronicle 28:20, David reminds Solomon that God would be with him as he finishes the work God called him to do.

> "Then David said to Solomon his son, "Be strong and courageous and do it. Do not be afraid and do not be dismayed, for the LORD God, even my God, is with you. He will not leave you or forsake you, until all the work for the service of the house of the LORD is finished."

We can rest assured that God will be with us in whatever He calls us to accomplish.

God promises us His presence. He does not promise that the world will become safer. When the disciples saw Jesus die, they cowered in a room for days, afraid that they too would be taken captive and killed. Yet, after Jesus rose from the dead, he appeared to them and said in John 14:27,

> "Peace I leave with you; my peace I give to you. Not as the world gives do I give to you. Let not your hearts be troubled, neither let them be afraid."

Jesus said this to them before he commissioned them to go and share the good news of salvation with others. There would be great risk, and many of them would eventually be martyrs for their faith, but Jesus promised He would give them peace as they stepped out in courage to share the gospel. In the United States, we do not need to fear the same persecution that the disciples faced, yet many of us fear sharing about Jesus with others. This fear prohibits us from obeying Jesus' command to make disciples. If we want to live as faithful disciples of Christ, we must gain a heart of courage.

When God isn't our focus, fear will take over. When we lack courage, we must go to God in prayer and read His Word.

Psalm 27:14 says,

> "Wait for the Lord; be strong, and let your heart take courage; wait for the Lord."

Psalm 34:4 says,

> "I sought the Lord, and he answered me and delivered me from all my fears."

It is in His presence that we find the peace and courage to move forward and do what God wants us to do. Our fearful hearts can be transformed into courageous hearts when we focus on God and not our circumstances.

> "Only do not rebel against the LORD. And do not fear the people of the land, for they are bread for us. Their protection is removed from them, and the LORD is with us; do not fear them." -Numbers 14:9

"Be strong and courageous. Do not fear or be in dread of them, for it is the LORD your God who goes with you. He will not leave you or forsake you." Then Moses summoned Joshua and said to him in the sight of all Israel, "Be strong and courageous, for you shall go with this people into the land that the LORD has sworn to their fathers to give them, and you shall put them in possession of it. It is the LORD who goes before you. He will be with you; he will not leave you or forsake you. Do not fear or be dismayed."
-Deuteronomy 31:6-8

"Be strong and courageous, for you shall cause this people to inherit the land that I swore to their fathers to give them. Only be strong and very courageous, being careful to do according to all the law that Moses my servant commanded you. Do not turn from it to the right hand or to the left, that you may have good success wherever you go."
-Joshua 1:6-7

"Be strong, and let your heart take courage, all you who wait for the Lord." -Psalm 31:24

TAKE A MOMENT

1. Where have you been focusing on your circumstances and not on God?

2. Where do you need courage to walk by faith and not by sight?

> *Heavenly Father, I do not want to live in fear. I want to live a life of faith, believing You are in control, and You are with me. I want to have the courage to step out and do what You want me to do. Help me not to fear people and courageously share Jesus with others. As I wait on You, please give me Your peace so that I can be a part of Kingdom building alongside You. Amen.*

DAY 28
JOYLESS HEART → JOY-FILLED HEART

No one is without moments of deep grief, pain, and loss. From King David to the Prophets, to Jesus Himself, grief is an emotion that will overwhelm all of us in certain seasons of our lives. The theme in the book Lamentations is grieving.

Lamentations 5:15 says,

> "The joy of our hearts has ceased; our dancing has been turned to mourning."

The prophet Jeremiah was known as "The weeping prophet" and said in chapter 8:18,

> "My joy is gone; grief is upon me; my heart is sick within me."

Grief is painful, but does it need to take away our joy?

Is it possible to experience joy while in mourning? Can we choose joy when walking through difficult trials? Isn't the gut-wrenching emotion of grief the opposite of joy? Or, can they be felt in tandem with each other? All things are possible with God, even joy, after the most painful of circumstances. We just need to know how to find it.

James 1:2-4 says,

> "Count it all joy, my brothers, when you meet trials of various kinds, for you know that the testing of your faith produces steadfastness. And let steadfastness have its full effect, that you may be perfect and complete, lacking in nothing."

James is challenging us to see our trails as a means of becoming more like Jesus. Though painful, God will transform us into His likeness. When we focus on Jesus, He will perfect our faith in trials and bring us hope. He modeled this when He faced the cross. His hope was set on His resurrection and sitting at the right hand of God having power over sin, Satan and death.

Hebrews 12:2 says,

> "Looking to Jesus, the founder and perfecter of our faith, who for the joy that was set before him endured the cross, despising the shame, and is seated at the right hand of the throne of God."

Our hope is that we are made righteous due to Jesus' sacrifice. Becoming righteous is the only way we can be in the presence of God. Having this hope should bring us joy.

Proverbs 10:28 says,

> "The hope of the righteous brings joy, but the expectation of the wicked will perish."

Joy comes when we grasp the precious and costly gift of our salvation. Maybe, like King David, we need to pray Psalm 51:12.

> "Restore to me the joy of your salvation, and uphold me with a willing spirit."

No matter the circumstances around us, we can choose to rejoice in the Lord and actively take joy in our salvation.

Habakkuk 3:17-18 says,

> "Though the fig tree should not blossom, nor fruit be on the vines, the produce of the olive fail, and the fields yield no food, the flock be cut off from the fold and there be no herd in the stalls, yet I will rejoice in the LORD; I will take joy in the God of my salvation."

Joy is a fruit of the Holy Spirit living inside of us.

Galatians 5:22-23 says,

> "But the fruit of the Spirit is love, joy, peace, patience, kindness, goodness, faithfulness, gentleness, self-control; against such things there is no law."

When we lack joy, we can ask the Holy Spirit to empower us to have joy in all circumstances and remember that there is hope.

Paul prayed this for the church in Rome in Romans 15:13,

> "May the God of hope fill you with all joy and peace in believing, so that by the power of the Holy Spirit you may abound in hope."

Jesus knew that there would be sorrows in life, but we can find joy in His presence. He said to His disciples in John 16:22,

> "So also you have sorrow now, but I will see you again, and your hearts will rejoice, and no one will take your joy from you."

Jesus sent us the Holy Spirit so that we can continually fellowship with God on this side of heaven. It is the Spirit who guides us and fills us with joy.

Psalm 16:11 says,

> "You make known to me the path of life; in your presence there is fullness of joy; at your right hand are pleasures forevermore."

We experience God's presence by reading His Word. When we hungrily devour the Word, we experience His love, gain proper perspective, and have hope, which brings us joy deep in our hearts.

Jeremiah 15:16 says,

> "Your words were found, and I ate them, and your words became to me a joy and the delight of my heart, for I am called by your name, O Lord, God of hosts."

Psalm 119:111 says,

> "Your testimonies are my heritage forever, for they are the joy of my heart."

When we spend time in the Word, we want to obey God by keeping His commandments. Our love for Him and His love for us brings us joy in knowing we are in good standing with Him.

John 15:10-11 says,

> "If you keep my commandments, you will abide in my love, just as I have kept my Father's commandments and abide in his love. These things I have spoken to you, that my joy may be in you, and that your joy may be full."

Psalm 97:11 reiterates that there is joy in obedience.

> "Light is sown for the righteous, and joy for the upright in heart."

When we sin, we can rest assured that if we confess our sins and turn from them, God will forgive us and joy will return.

Psalm 30:4-5 says,

> "Sing praises to the LORD, O you his saints, and give thanks to his holy name. For his anger is but for a moment, and his favor is for a lifetime. Weeping may tarry for the night, but joy comes with the morning."

Nothing can steal our joy when we are thankful for our salvation, when the Spirit empowers us, and when we are experiencing His presence by being obedient to His Word. Joy will come in the morning if our hearts are focused on Him.

> "For the kingdom of God is not a matter of eating and drinking but of righteousness and peace and joy in the Holy Spirit." -Romans 14:17
>
> "In this you rejoice, though now for a little while, if necessary, you have been grieved by various trials, so that the tested genuineness of your faith—more precious than gold that perishes though it is tested by fire—may be found to result in praise and glory and honor at the revelation of Jesus Christ. Though you have not seen him, you love him. Though you do not now see him, you believe in him and rejoice with joy that is inexpressible and filled with glory,obtaining the outcome of your faith, the salvation of your souls."
> -1 Peter 1:6-9
>
> "Splendor and majesty are before him; strength and joy are in his place." -1 Chronicles 16:27
>
> "The meek shall obtain fresh joy in the LORD, and the poor among mankind shall exult in the Holy One of Israel."
> -Isaiah 29:19

"Offer right sacrifices, and put your trust in the LORD. There are many who say, "Who will show us some good? Lift up the light of your face upon us, O LORD!" You have put more joy in my heart than they have when their grain and wine abound." -Psalm 4:5-7

"His master said to him, 'Well done, good and faithful servant. You have been faithful over a little; I will set you over much. Enter into the joy of your master.'"
-Matthew 25:23

"For you make him most blessed forever; you make him glad with the joy of your presence." -Psalm 21:6

"For to the one who pleases him God has given wisdom and knowledge and joy, but to the sinner he has given the business of gathering and collecting, only to give to one who pleases God. This also is vanity and a striving after wind."
-Ecclesiastes 2:26

TAKE A MOMENT

1. How can you still focus on joy in times of trials or grief?

2. What distracts you from going to the Word and experiencing God's presence in times of trials?

> *Heavenly Father, thank You for the joy of my salvation. May I never take it for granted. Thank You for Your Word, where I can experience Your presence and learn how to obey You. Thank You for the Holy Spirit, who will give me joy when I ask. Amen.*

DAY 29

FOOLISH HEART → WISE HEART

God created us to feel emotions. Some of us may seem to be more aware of our emotions than others, but that's not the point. God gave us feelings because we wouldn't experience His love without them. His love is what centers us. His love is what gives us peace, comfort and hope. God gives us emotions to experience intimacy with Him and others.

God also gave us a mind to think. Some of us may seem to have more brains than others, but that's not the point either. God gave us a mind to learn His wisdom so that we know how to direct our thoughts and emotions rather than be directed by them.

Proverbs 23:19 says,

> "Hear, my son, and be wise, and direct your heart in the way."

Proverbs 14:8 says,

> "The wisdom of the prudent is to discern his way, but the folly of fools is deceiving."

God gave us a mind to learn from Him what is wise and then direct our thoughts and emotions toward that end.

Though our emotions and minds were given to us by God, they are not naturally wise due to our sinful nature. We are stubbornly foolish. Our hearts do not protect us. We cannot trust our thoughts and feelings to be wise in and of themselves. Our hearts can lead us astray to dishonor God as well as our bodies.

Romans 1:21 says,

> "For although they knew God, they did not honor him as God or give thanks to him, but they became futile in their thinking, and their foolish hearts were darkened."

We might know God, but are we going to Him with our thoughts and emotions to see what we should do and how to respond? Or, do we put Him on the back burner, allowing our minds to wander unchecked and our emotions to run wild without restraints so that our hearts lead us off of God's path for us?

When we follow our hearts and the lust that lies within, we will walk away from the light of life and live in the darkness of sin.

Romans 1 continues in verse 24,

> "Therefore God gave them up in the lusts of their hearts to impurity, to the dishonoring of their bodies among themselves."

At some point, we will stop feeling the conviction of the Holy Spirit if we continue to follow our emotions, feelings, and desires instead of God and His Word. The world says to us: "Just do it." "Do what feels right in your heart." "Do what you think is right." "If it's not hurting someone, it's alright." "If it's love, it's not sinning." "If it feels good, it must be good!" This is the world's wisdom, not God's. If we continue to follow this advice, we cannot protect ourselves from sin, Satan, and our self-destructive behaviors.

We cannot obtain wisdom from within ourselves. Wisdom is only from God.

Job 12:13 says,

> "With God are wisdom and might; he has counsel and understanding."

He is our best counselor. He will give us the proper understanding of what we should do. Job continues in 15:8, "Have you listened in the council of God? And do you limit wisdom to yourself?"

Proverbs 28:26 says we are a fool if we listen only to ourselves and don't seek God.

> "Whoever trusts in his own mind is a fool, but he who walks in wisdom will be delivered."

When we fear God, honoring Him as all-knowing, perfectly holy, and all-wise, we will run to Him for His counsel before we move forward. To grow in wisdom, we must first grow in our fear of the Lord.

Job 28:28 says,

> "And he said to man, 'Behold, the fear of the Lord, that is wisdom, and to turn away from evil is understanding.'"

Proverbs 1:7 says,

> "The fear of the LORD is the beginning of knowledge; fools despise wisdom and instruction."

When we fear the Lord, we will run to Him for instructions on what to do and not act impulsively at the moment.

Wisdom is given to us by the Holy Spirit.

Isaiah 11:2 says,

> "And the Spirit of the LORD shall rest upon him, the Spirit of wisdom and understanding, the Spirit of counsel and might, the Spirit of knowledge and the fear of the LORD."

1 Corinthians 2:13 goes on to say,

> "And we impart this in words not taught by human wisdom but taught by the Spirit, interpreting spiritual truths to those who are spiritual."

The Spirit has all wisdom. We just need to ask Him to impart it to us.

James 1:5 says,

> "If any of you lacks wisdom, let him ask God, who gives generously to all without reproach, and it will be given him."

Proverbs 2:6-7 says,

> "For the LORD gives wisdom; from his mouth come knowledge and understanding; he stores up sound wisdom for the upright; he is a shield to those who walk in integrity."

Following God's wisdom protects us.

To grow in wisdom, we must grow in discerning what is right and wrong according to the Bible, not by what we feel or think.

James 3:17 tells us what wisdom is,

> "But the wisdom from above is first pure, then peaceable, gentle, open to reason, full of mercy and good fruits, impartial and sincere."

If what we are about to do or say is not on this list, we would be foolish to move forward.

Proverbs 4:5 encourages us to

> "Get wisdom; get insight; do not forget, and do not turn away from the words of my mouth."

If we aren't learners when it comes to the knowledge of God, then we will become futile in our thinking, unable to produce any useful result with our lives.

When we find wisdom and live it out, we know we have hope and a future.

Proverbs 24:14 says,

> "Know that wisdom is such to your soul; if you find it, there will be a future, and your hope will not be cut off."

There is no future for a fool. Fools continue in their folly which will lead to destruction. Let us intentionally pursue wisdom in God's Word so that we will make wise choices and have a future that is blessed.

> "For wisdom will come into your heart, and knowledge will be pleasant to your soul." -Proverbs 2:10

> "An intelligent heart acquires knowledge, and the ear of the wise seeks knowledge." -Proverbs 18:15

> "So teach us to number our days that we may get a heart of wisdom." -Psalm 90:12

> "The fear of the LORD is the beginning of wisdom; all those who practice it have a good understanding. His praise endures forever!" -Psalm 111:10

> "Wisdom rests in the heart of a man of understanding, but it makes itself known even in the midst of fools."
> -Proverbs 14:33

> "Behold, you delight in truth in the inward being, and you teach me wisdom in the secret heart." -Psalm 51:6

"The wise of heart is called discerning, and sweetness of speech increases persuasiveness." -Proverbs 16:21

"I do not cease to give thanks for you, remembering you in my prayers, that the God of our Lord Jesus Christ, the Father of glory, may give you the Spirit of wisdom and of revelation in the knowledge of him, having the eyes of your hearts enlightened, that you may know what is the hope to which he has called you, what are the riches of his glorious inheritance in the saints, and what is the immeasurable greatness of his power toward us who believe, according to the working of his great might." -Ephesians 1:16-19

TAKE A MOMENT

1. What thoughts and emotions do you need to take to God to learn how to respond correctly?

2. What would it look like for you to intentionally seek God for wisdom in certain areas of your life?

> *Heavenly Father, thank You for offering me Your wisdom if I ask for it. Thank You that the Holy Spirit will guide me in Your Word to know the right way to think and manage my emotions in all circumstances. Help me to not be deceived by my thoughts and feelings, but to pause and take them to You for any needed corrections before I proceed. Amen.*

DAY 30

HARD HEART → COMPASSIONATE HEART

Hardened hearts are like callouses. A callous can rarely feel anything. Part of its purpose is to protect the sensitive skin underneath from experiencing the constant pain of friction. A callous numbs hidden pain by creating a thick pad of dead skin cells. The thick pad isn't formed in one day. It's developed after repeated irritation on the skin. Calluses are usually ignored or forgotten until they split open and get infected. The infection can spread to the bone or the blood. If our blood gets infected, we can get blood poisoning or sepsis and die. Just like an infected callous, a hard heart infects our entire life. It can destroy us and our relationships if we don't take care of it.

One area we may be calloused in is the expectations and boundaries given to us in God's Word. When God's commands rub us the wrong way, we can acquire a callused heart that is no longer sensitive to the ways of God. We may stop feeling convicted about areas the Bible clearly says are sin because we have allowed the world and its values to rub us long enough to callous our hearts.

Ephesians 4:18-19 says,

> "They are darkened in their understanding, alienated from the life of God because of the ignorance that is in them, due to their hardness of heart. They have become callous and have given themselves up to sensuality, greedy to practice every kind of impurity."

Our hearts are enticed by the lusts of the flesh, the lusts of the eyes, and the boastful pride of life *(1 John 2:15-17)*. We may callous our hearts by watching shows with explicit sensual content or looking at inappropriate pictures. Or we may callous our hearts toward being good stewards of our finances by living above our means and being in debt. God says we should have no outstanding debt in Romans 13:8.

Over time, even the church has grown calloused to specific topics in the Bible that Jesus addressed. One area that Jesus called out the religious leaders on was the area of divorce. Back in Jesus' time, the Jewish men thought it was permissible for them to divorce their wives for any and every reason. This is the view of divorce in our country today. We believe we can have any reason to end the covenant we made before God about our commitment to our spouse.

Jesus answered the religious officials with a shocking answer in Matthew 19:8-9.

> "He said to them, 'Because of your hardness of heart Moses allowed you to divorce your wives, but from the beginning it was not so. And I say to you: whoever divorces your wife, except for sexual immorality, and marries another, commits adultery.'"

The Jewish law allowed divorce because the people's hearts were hardened. This meant they were self-centered and unloving toward their spouse. This law was given to protect the women in Jewish society. Jesus emphasized that God's law doesn't approve divorce or even require it where there is infidelity. Jesus reminded the religious leaders that God's intentions for marriage were for a man and women to live together in faithfulness and love for their lifetime. This means couples would need to grow in compassion and humility. We'd need to grow into being servants of one another and learn how to submit to one another. We'd need to listen, learn, and lean into our spouse's interests and not just our own.

We might become defensive and say, "But what about if they cheated on me? What if they are abusive? What if they are stuck in destructive addiction?" These are serious challenges, and even Jesus wanted individuals to be protected and not abused in marriages. Yet, when we look at the top 10 reasons for divorce, these aren't always why people run to the courtroom. The number one reason people divorce is over money issues. The second is a lack of intimacy with each other. The third and fourth are infidelity and abuse respectfully, but then we have a lack of compatibility and personal appearance of the partner. Addiction is seventh on the list. The last three are: got married too early, got married for the wrong reasons, and lack of communication. Most of these reasons are due to a hardness of heart, not because an individual is protecting themselves from abuse.

Hard hearts lose a sense of compassion and empathy toward others. When our hearts have friction with others, we begin to build walls to protect ourselves from emotional hurt. We give up on working through the difficult areas of communication, conflict resolution, and value differences, because we don't want to be hurt again. Instead of compassionately pursuing reconciliation and restoration, becoming more of a listener and learner, we push them away. We avoid. We see their faults, and they disgust us. Unforgiveness creeps in. Bitterness gets rooted in our calloused hearts, and we start to justify our actions. "We bring out the worst in each other." "We are on two different paths." "We aren't compatible." "We aren't in love anymore." "We'd be better apart." The next thing we know, divorce papers are on the table. "Till death do us part" is no longer seen as a covenant but a statement that was said in the blissful moments of young love that can be done away with for any reason.

The most important person to have compassion for is our spouse. It is a daily choice to put on a compassionate heart when our hearts want to only think of ourselves and become callous to others' words and actions. What if we were to intentionally live out Colossians 3:12-14 in our marriages and friendships?

Colossians 3:12-14 says,

> "Put on then, as God's chosen ones, holy and beloved, compassionate hearts, kindness, humility, meekness and patience, bearing with one another and, if one has a complaint against another, forgiving each other as the Lord has forgiven you, so you also must forgive. And above all these put on love, which binds everything together in perfect harmony."

When we allow bitterness, resentment, and hatred to enter into the cracks of our hearts, we are on the road to destruction. Our hardened hearts will play a part in ending relationships if we aren't willing to put on: compassion, kindness, humility, patience, forgiveness and love. Calloused hearts require intense surgery. When we ask the Holy Spirit to empower us with these character traits, our hearts can grow compassion and love. It's not a promise that relationships will be reconciled. Still, no matter what the other person decides, we can know our hearts were filled with the hope of reconciliation and restoration and that we tried to live like Jesus by having hearts of compassion.

> "When he saw the crowds, he had compassion for them, because they were harassed and helpless, like sheep without a shepherd." -Matthew 9:36

TAKE A MOMENT

1. Are you at a place where you will allow the Great Surgeon to take your calloused heart and replace it with a heart of compassion?

2. Who do you need to have more compassion toward? Pray God will give you the qualities found in Colossians 3 so that if a relationship does end, you know you were living as much like Jesus as possible.

> *Heavenly Father, I need You to take my calloused heart and turn it into a heart of compassion toward the people that have hurt me and are hard to love. Help me, through the power of the Holy Spirit, to be kind, humble, patient, forgiving, and loving. Help me to walk through the valleys of my relationships with You by my side. Grow my character in these trials. Protect me from bitterness, hatred, and unforgiveness. You were able to have compassion for sinners. Help me to do the same. Amen.*

DAY 31

LUSTFUL HEART → PURE HEART

It can feel hopeless at times to try to keep our ways pure. Everything in our culture is sexualized, be it video games, movies, advertisements on billboards, novels, magazines, or the halftime shows in the Super Bowl. Sex entices. Sex seduces. Sex entraps us. And it's everywhere.

One of the secret sins of the heart is lust. Lust is a psychological force producing an intense desire for someone or something. We can lust over things like money and power, not just people. Lust is sinful even though it's internal because we allow our impulsive urges to govern our thoughts and actions instead of controlling our thoughts so that we don't act on what we are thinking about.

Jesus said in Matthew 5:28,

> "But I say to you that everyone who looks at a woman with a lustful intent has already committed adultery with her in his heart."

Just the thought of being sexual with someone who is not our spouse is just like committing adultery! Lusting after others is being unfaithful with our eyes. Looking at a man or woman and thinking about them sexually is not respecting and honoring them. It's seeing them as an object and not a person. People are made in the image of God and should be valued as such. No one should be wanted only for their external appearance.

1 Samuel 16:7 says,

> "Man looks on the outward appearance, but the Lord looks on the heart."

If we don't learn how to control the lustful thoughts that come into our minds, God will stop convicting us.

Romans 1:24 says,

> "Therefore God gave them up in the lusts of their hearts to impurity, to the dishonoring of their bodies among themselves."

How do we dishonor our bodies? We send to others pictures of ourselves of body parts only our spouses should see. We fulfill ourselves sexually instead of fulfilling our sexual longings inside of marriage. We engage in intimacy with others outside of marriage. This will significantly affect our intimacy inside our marriage, even if we aren't married yet. The thoughts of our intimate relationships outside of marriage will not disappear once we are married. Our secret sins affect us and those we will get married to or are married to.

We must guard our purity as if we are a soldier protecting a great treasure of the king. We are that great treasure.

2 Timothy 2:22 says,

> "So flee youthful passions and pursue righteousness, faith, love and peace, along with those who call on the Lord from a pure heart."

Our first step is to flee any situation that we know might entice us to sin sexually. Suppose our eyes glance at an attractive individual. In that case, we need to look away, walk in the other direction, and immediately remind our minds that that gorgeous individual is made in the image of God and is to be valued and respected.

Our second step is to seek God in prayer and remind ourselves of scripture to focus on what is right and true and not allowing our thoughts to wander or daydream.

Psalm 119:9-11 says,

> "How can a young man keep his way pure? By guarding it according to your word. With my whole heart I seek you; let me not wander from your commands! I have stored up your word in my heart that I might not sin against you."

The Holy Spirit will empower us with self-control if we ask Him to do so. We invite Him to control us when we feel like our thoughts and emotions are out of control. Then, we think about God's commands.

A good verse is 1 Peter 1:22,

> "Having purified your souls by your obedience to the truth for a sincere brotherly love, love one another earnestly from a pure heart."

This verse reminds us that there is a way to love others with a pure heart, not a lustful heart. We are encouraged that every time we chose to obey God, we are not only becoming purer in our hearts, but we will be able to love others we are attracted to in an earnest, God-honoring way!

Pursuing a pure heart by turning away from temptation, inviting the Holy Spirit to give us self-control, and then filling our minds with scripture will not only honor the people around us but will enable us to love them in a way that is respectful and pure. Isn't that the way we all want to be loved?

> "A perverse heart shall be far from me; I will know nothing of evil." -Psalm 101:4

> "Do not desire her beauty in your heart, and do not let her capture you with her eyelashes." -Proverbs 6:25

“Let not your heart turn aside to her ways; do not stray into her paths.” -Proverbs 7:25

“He who loves purity of heart, and whose speech is gracious, will have the king as his friend.” -Proverbs 22:11

“Blessed are the pure in heart, for they shall see God.” -Matthew 5:8

TAKE A MOMENT

1. Where are you most tempted to fall into lustful thinking?

2. Why is it essential for you to fight for a pure heart now? What is at stake if you don't?

> *Heavenly Father, please help me to honor and respect the people around me that I find attractive. Help me to see them from a pure heart and not a lustful one. When my eyes want to linger, help me look away. Help my mind immediately ask for the Holy Spirit to give me self-control, and may I focus on scripture to provide me with the strength to pursue purity. Amen.*

DAY 32
IDOLATROUS HEART → SURRENDERED HEART

Have you ever tried to pry a forbidden, unsafe object from a toddler's hands? Their hands clench. Their face is red with anger. They voice the one word they know how to say so well, "NO!" It is frustrating as the guardian to know that you must get this dangerous object out of the child's hands to keep him safe, even though he will never understand why.

This is how we are toward God. He knows we hold on too tightly to certain things that can harm us. Yet, when He offers to protect and guide us to safety, we get angry. We do not want to surrender certain things. We believe they will bring us comfort. They will bring us joy. They will provide love and stability.

Our hopes are set on a particular relationship working out, a career path coming to fruition, having the home of our dreams, and experiencing exotic vacations. We believe a specific position will give us power. A certain person will provide us with love. A specific career will provide us with a purpose. Though each of these things isn't bad in and of themselves, they can be dangerous if we put them as the focus in our hearts rather than God. If these goals or desires are placed higher than intimacy with Christ, then we are cultivating an idolatrous heart.

2 Chronicles 20:33 says,

> "The high places, however, were not taken away; the people had not yet set their hearts upon the God of their fathers."

We must choose who or what we place as the highest priority and focus in our lives.

What does God want us to surrender to Him freely?

1 Chronicles 29:17 says,

> "I know, my God that you test the heart and have pleasure in uprightness. In the uprightness of my heart I have freely offered all these things, and now I have seen your people, who are present here, offering freely and joyously to you."

He wants us to be willing to surrender all things to Him.

Surrender is scary unless we understand that God asks us to surrender things because He cares for us. He cares about what might be hurting us or harming us. He cares about our potential. He cares about us becoming more like Jesus, which means letting go of things that are not making us pure. Our first step toward surrender must be to choose to trust God based on His character, not our own wisdom.

We must trust God enough to surrender our agendas, reputations, expectations, relationships, possessions and follow Him. We may never know exactly why He's asking us to give up this one particular thing, especially if it doesn't seem wrong or harmful, but we still must trust that He asks us to surrender things for our greater good.

We must love God enough to say that we want to do His will more than our own will. Our love and trust for Him will be our motivators when surrender is painful and seemingly impossible at the moment. When letting go of something feels like death: the death of a relationship, death of a dream, death of a career; when saying yes to following Him means ridicule, persecution, and sacrifice; when surrender feels like all joy, hope and peace has been sucked out of us and been replaced by uncertainty, grief, and some anxiety. We surrender, not because it feels good or right, but because we love Him.

Jesus is not asking us to do something He didn't do. Jesus surrendered to God the Father's plan when He prayed in the garden before He was arrested to be taken to His death.

Jesus said in Luke 22:42,

> "Father, not my will, but yours be done."

Jesus had to trust that God the Father's plan was the best way to accomplish saving us. It was not a painless solution. It was excruciating physically, emotionally, relationally, and spiritually. Jesus experienced all aspects of pain for us to have the opportunity to be reconciled to the Father.

We cannot expect to surrender and not experience any loss, suffering, or pain. It is through surrendering that we become more like Jesus in His death. We must put to death whatever God asks, so that, we can truly experience the life He has for us. When we surrender, we also experience the power of the Holy Spirit working through us to bring new life within ourselves and to others around us.

The apostle Paul knew this trade-off very well: In Philippians 3:7-8, he said,

> "But whatever gain I had, I counted as loss for the sake of Christ. Indeed, I count everything as loss because of the surpassing worth of knowing Christ Jesus my Lord. For His sake, I have suffered the loss of all things and count them as rubbish, in order that I may gain Christ and be found in him."

We must have a greater vision about surrender. It is not about what we are losing or that it will be hard, which is true, but that we will gain so much more if we surrender. We will gain Christ. We will experience Him more fully. We will have a deeper joy, a greater peace, a richer fulfillment in our lives because we are living for Him and His purposes and not ourselves.

Let us release what we've been holding on to and

> "Let us lift up our hearts and hands to God in Heaven."
> -Lamentations 3:41

May we remove the idols of our hearts in surrender so we can experience His incredible will for our lives.

> "And he did what was right in the eyes of the Lord, yet not with a whole heart." -2 Chronicles 25:2

> "Let your heart therefore be wholly true to the Lord our God, walking in his statues and keeping his commandments, as at this day." -1 Kings 8:61

TAKE A MOMENT

1. What things have you placed before God in your life?

2. How does thinking about what Jesus' surrender cost Him help you be open to the cost of surrender?

> *Heavenly Father, show me areas in my life that I have prioritized over You. Show me what You want me to surrender. Help me to love and trust You enough to be willing to surrender anything You ask me to surrender. I open my heart and hands to You as Lord of my life and my first priority. Amen.*

DAY 33

CONDEMNING HEART → CONTRITE HEART

How we were parented as a child can often affect how we view God as an adult. If our parents gave us too much freedom and didn't give us boundaries or rules, we might have enjoyed our freedom to sin as a child or teenager. We experienced continual grace with no truth or consequences. This hinders our hearts from grasping how sin affects us and others. We might think as an adult that God doesn't care if we sin here and there, as long as it doesn't seem to be hurting others.

If we were raised with lots of rules and consequences, rather than principles to learn how to make wise decisions on our own, we might live in fear and condemnation. We might remember our parents saying, "Shame on you!" or, "I can't even look at you, I'm so disappointed!" or, "Why would you be so stupid?" Those hurtful words, said in frustration and anger, leave a mark on our hearts. We feel rejected, leaving us with little hope to regain trust and intimacy. We become people-pleasers with our hearts living in fear of rejection. We experience condemnation in our hearts and think that God, too, must be condemning us.

If we were raised by parents who led out of grace, showing love and acceptance when we messed up, as well as truth to learn there are appropriate consequences for our choices, we will have lived in a secure relationship with them. We would know that even when we make bad choices, our parents will help train and guide us, but we will still need to take responsibility for what we've done. This gives us a healthier view of God as adults. We know we will mess up, but we can always go to Him for His forgiveness, mercy and grace. There may be ramifications for our bad choices, but God will still walk through the journey with us.

God the Father is a God of justice. Sin will be condemned. That is why He sent Jesus to die on the cross for our sins. He wanted us to experience His grace and mercy, not His wrath. Jesus was full of both grace and truth *(John 1:14)*. Jesus came, not to condemn, but to seek and save the lost. When we put our faith and trust in Jesus, we no longer need to fear the wrath of God. Our sin will still have consequences on this side of eternity, but when we go before our Heavenly Father, He will see us as pure and righteous because of Jesus.

Even though God will no longer condemn us, our hearts and thoughts sometimes will.

1 John 3:19-20 says,

> "By this we shall know that we are of the truth and reassure our heart before him; for whenever our heart condemns us, God is greater than our heart, and he knows everything."

Romans 2:15 says,

> "They show that the work of the law is written on their hearts, while their conscience also bears witness, and their conflicting thoughts accuse or even excuse them."

If God says He has forgiven us because of Jesus' sacrifice, then we must believe Him. Jesus died an excruciating, humiliating death to pay for all of our sins. He took on the wrath of God so that we don't ever have to experience it. If we continue to live in guilt, shame, and condemnation, we insult Christ and His sacrifice on the cross.

God does not want us to condemn ourselves when we sin, but He does want us to have a contrite heart toward sin. A contrite heart shows sincere remorse over what we've done and a desire to make it right through repentance. Sin grieves God and harms others even though it is forgiven. Sin still has consequences for us and our relationships.

Psalm 51:17 says,

> "The sacrifices of God are a broken spirit; a broken and contrite heart, O God, you will not despise."

Freedom and forgiveness come when our hearts are broken over our sin, and we turn toward God. Our contrite hearts lead us to repentance and to turn from our sinful ways, never wanting to return to that sinful state again. A contrite heart revives us because we know that God graciously accepts us into His loving presence now and for all eternity.

Isaiah 57:15 says,

> "For thus says the One who is high and lifted up, who inhabits eternity, whose name is Holy: 'I dwell in the high and holy place, and also with him who is of a contrite and lowly spirit, to revive the spirit of the lowly, and to revive the heart of the contrite.'"

No matter our upbringing, let us no longer live in condemnation.

Romans 8:1 says,

> "There is therefore now no condemnation for those who are in Christ Jesus."

Let our hearts be sensitive to our sin so that we are quick to be reconciled to God so we can experience His love, grace, and mercy.

> "Look, O Lord, for I am in distress; my stomach churns; my heart is wrung within me, because I have been very rebellious. In the street the sword bereaves; in the house it is like death." -Lamentations 1:20

“Concerning the prophets: My heart is broken within me; all my bones shake; I am like a drunken man, like a man overcome by wine, because of the Lord and because of his holy words.” -Jeremiah 23:9

“My heart throbs; my strength fails me, and the light of my eyes- it also has gone from me.” -Psalm 38:10

TAKE A MOMENT

1. Where have you felt self-condemnation that you need to let go of at the cross?

2. What area do you need to have a contrite heart so that you can experience God's forgiveness and presence in your life?

> *Heavenly Father, thank You that You are full of grace and truth. You lovingly convict me of sin, but because of Christ, You do not condemn me. Help me to have a contrite heart to be sensitive to sin and be quick to repent. May I experience Your love, grace, and mercy so that I can live in Your presence now and for all eternity. Amen.*

DAY 34
SERVING HEART

Life is busy. Whether you are a business owner trying to keep your business afloat, a stay at home mom trying to keep the kids and house in order, or a college student trying to pass all of your classes, there never seems to be enough time to do all that we feel we need to do or want to do. Our hearts can get weary with the day-to-day responsibilities in life, and so when we hear that we are to have a serving heart, it just seems like too much.

Jesus lived a different sort of life. He came to seek and save the lost. He came to serve those around Him by providing for their immediate needs and dying for their spiritual needs. Jesus never was in a hurry or stressed out, though He did get tired. That's when He went away to spend time with the Father. That is how He renewed His strength to continue to serve. His purpose in coming to earth was to be a servant. He was a servant during His life and a servant in His death. Jesus was able to do this because He was focused on two things: accomplishing God's work while on earth and bringing God glory.

He said in His final prayer in John 17:4,

> "I glorified you on earth, having accomplished the work that you gave me to do."

Just as Jesus was a servant, He instructed His disciples to see themselves as servants.

Matthew 20:25-28 says,

> "But Jesus called them to him and said, "You know that the rulers of the Gentiles lord it over them, and their great ones exercise authority over them. It shall not be so among you. But whoever would be great among you must be your servant, and whoever would be first among you must be

> your slave, even as the Son of Man came not to be served but to serve, and to give his life as a ransom for many."

We are often busy, overwhelmed and stressed because we are serving whatever builds our kingdom. We think we need to work harder. We need to kiss-up to teachers, employers or potential clients. We spend so much energy focused on moving forward in this temporal life that we forget that our focus is to be on the eternal: serving God in all that we do to bring Him glory.

Luke 4:8 says,

> "And Jesus answered him, "It is written, "'You shall worship the Lord your God, and him only shall you serve.'"

We need to evaluate if we are serving God or serving whatever makes us more money.

Matthew 6:24 emphasizes this,

> "No one can serve two masters, for either he will hate the one and love the other, or he will be devoted to the one and despise the other. You cannot serve God and money."

Our focus needs to shift from serving ourselves by building our kingdoms to serving God and building His Kingdom.

Daniel 7:14 says,

> "And to him was given dominion and glory and a kingdom, that all peoples, nations, and languages should serve him; his dominion is an everlasting dominion, which shall not pass away, and his kingdom one that shall not be destroyed."

No one is exempt from serving God and His Kingdom. What we invest in toward God's Kingdom will never be destroyed or taken away.

God has given us different personalities, passions, and giftings to serve God and others. Though how we serve God might differ, we all serve for the same purpose in mind: for God to be glorified.

1 Peter 4:10-11 says,

> "As each has received a gift, use it to serve one another, as good stewards of God's varied grace: whoever speaks, as one who speaks oracles of God; whoever serves, as one who serves by the strength that God supplies—in order that in everything God may be glorified through Jesus Christ. To him belong glory and dominion forever and ever. Amen."

We glorify God by living for eternity while we are here on earth. People will notice how we serve God and others, and they will see we are different from the world.

Some of us might wonder if we are disqualified from serving the Lord due to sins we've committed in the past. Even when we've done wrong, God can still use us for His Kingdom.

1 Samuel 12:20 says,

> "And Samuel said to the people, 'Do not be afraid; you have done all this evil. Yet do not turn aside from following the Lord, but serve the Lord with all your heart.'"

God doesn't use sinless people to be His servants. He uses repentant people willing to follow Him moving forward. God uses imperfect people so that He gets the most glory.

When our hearts become serving hearts, we will not only be modeling Jesus' heart toward others, but we will have a clearer, more fulfilling purpose in life. The career we have to make money is no longer the focus. How to serve others to bring God glory in that career becomes the greater focus. We are blessed when we look for ways to be a blessing. That's how we are transformed from the inside out.

> "And you, Solomon my son, know the God of your father and serve him with a whole heart and with a willing mind, for the Lord searches all hearts and understands every plan and thought. If you seek him, he will be found by you, but if you forsake him, he will cast you off forever."
> -1 Chronicles 28:9
>
> "Serve the LORD with fear, and rejoice with trembling."
> -Psalms 2:11
>
> "For you were called to freedom, brothers. Only do not use your freedom as an opportunity for the flesh, but through love serve one another." -Galatians 5:13

TAKE A MOMENT

1. How do you need to change your thinking on what having a servant's heart looks like in your family, career, and community?

2. How might God be asking you to serve Him in your career and let go of the stress of making more money?

> *Heavenly Father, help me to focus on serving You and not myself. Show me how to invest in Your eternal Kingdom and not my temporal kingdom. Show me who to serve in my family, at my work, and where I play. May I serve with a faithful, glad heart to bring You glory! Amen.*

DAY 35
SINCERE HEART

When we go to work each day, we may see it as a means of just making money. Maybe your job brings great joy and fulfillment, but that is not always the case. You may work for an employer who doesn't necessarily care about you. They may care only about getting the job done and done well. Yesterday, we talked about having a serving heart. Serving is not just in our voluntary activities like PTSO's, kids' sports, or serving at church. Having a serving heart is just as important in our jobs. It's not about getting a task done to fulfill our responsibilities; it's about doing them with a sincere heart. We are to sincerely care that our work gets done and done rightly. Our hearts become healthier when we serve with a sincere heart, even when our work is expected of us and not necessarily appreciated.

The Bible compares us to being bondservants. A bondservant works without wages, literally, a slave. Being under the authority of another may not only feel oppressive, but it may also feel devaluing. Jesus saw being a bondservant differently. He taught that those who would be most significant in God's kingdom took on the role of a servant while here on earth. It's wise to choosethe position of a servant in life.

In Mark 9:35, He said,

> "If anyone would be first, he must be last of all and servant of all."

It is counter-cultural to say we want to be a servant more than a leader. We are to submit ourselves under earthly authority and care about others' needs first. Our fleshly hearts will fight against this concept because it is ingrained in us to be independent, question authority, and care about our rights and freedoms.

God wants us to treat our employers with respect. He wants us to do our jobs sincerely, not to try to gain the approval of our leaders, but to bring glory to God. We are to have goodwill toward those we are employed by, even if they don't deserve it. We can only do this when we change our perspective that we are not serving people but God.

Ephesians 6:5-8 says,

> "Bondservants, obey your earthly masters with fear and trembling, with a sincere heart, as you would Christ, not by the way of eye-service, as people-pleasers, but as bondservants of Christ, doing the will of God from the heart, rendering service with a good will as to the Lord and not to man, knowing that whatever good anyone does, this he will receive back from the Lord, whether he is a bondservant or is free."

There will be a reward from God for how we sincerely do our jobs, no matter the approval, affirmation, or attention we receive from our leaders.

Our hearts can become critical or judgmental of those who lead us. We think we know how to do it better. We believe we have a better strategy. That is not the role God gives us. God puts them in charge and will hold them accountable for how well they do their job at leading us and leading the company. Our role is to do what is expected of us with a sincere heart.

There may come a time that we need to have a conversation with our employers. How we lead out in that conversation matters. When we approach them with sincere concern and gentleness, being for them in the conversation instead of against them, we just might be able to draw them away from the destructiveness of their own hearts.

2 Timothy 2:24-26 says,

> "And the Lord's servant must not be quarrelsome but kind to everyone, able to teach, patiently enduring evil, correcting his opponents with gentleness. God may perhaps grant them repentance leading to a knowledge of the truth, and they may come to their senses and escape from the snare of the devil, after being captured by him to do his will."

When our employers see we sincerely care, we can significantly impact them toward being open to the gospel. Remember, they are sinners in need of a Savior too.

Our attitude in serving is crucial. If we serve begrudgingly, inconsistently, or look stressed and overwhelmed when we serve, our actions will just look like any other person in the workforce, and we will have no impact on those we work for or with.

Psalm 100:2 says,

> "Serve the LORD with gladness! Come into his presence with singing!"

Romans 12:11 adds,

> "Do not be slothful in zeal, be fervent in spirit, serve the Lord."

1 Samuel 12:24 says,

> "Only fear the Lord and serve him faithfully with all your heart. For consider what great things he has done for you."

We are first and foremost servants of Christ. The best way to serve Christ is to serve our earthly leaders with sincere, submissive, respectful hearts. When we have our minds set on Him and work sincerely for the Lord, we will be a blessing to others and have an opportunity to make an impact in their lives.

One of the benefits of intentionally working toward transforming our hearts is that we can come alongside others on their transformation journey. One of the most significant ways we can do that is to sincerely serve others with love and respect.

> "Bondservants, obey in everything those who are your earthly masters, not by way of eye-service, as people pleasers, but with sincerity of heart, fearing the Lord." -Colossians 3:22

> "But in your hearts honor Christ the Lord as holy, always being prepared to make a defense to anyone who asks you for a reason for the hope that is in you; yet do it with gentleness and respect." -1 Peter 3:15

TAKE A MOMENT

1. When is it difficult to serve sincerely at your work?

2. How can having the perspective that you are serving the Lord and not just your employer help you to have a better attitude as you work?

> *Heavenly Father, please give me eyes to see my employers as people in need of Your mercy and grace. Help me to sincerely serve them so that I can have an opportunity to share the gospel with them. Remind me daily that I am working for You and Your glory, not their approval or recognition. Holy Spirit empower me to love and be a blessing with those I work with. Amen.*

DAY 36
REPENTANT HEART

We have been deeply evaluating our hearts for five weeks. If you have come this far and taken steps to allow God to do surgery on your heart, then you are already a different person. You have been intentionally rebuilding, restoring, and renewing your heart.

Isaiah 61:4 says,

> "They will rebuild the ancient ruins and restore the places long devastated; they will renew the ruined cities that have been devastated for generations."

Your heart is being rebuilt on the foundation of God's Word. Your heart is being restored to its proper function and health. Your heart is being renewed by the power of the Holy Spirit, convicting you, sanctifying you, and giving you the ability to think and do what is right.

But what happens when this devotional is finished, and we move on to some other focus? What should we do when our hearts deceive us again, and Christ is no longer our first devotion?

Revelation 2:4-5 says,

> "But I have this against you, that you have abandoned the love you had at first. Remember therefore from where you have fallen; repent, and do the works you did at first. If not, I will come to you and remove your lampstand from its place, unless you repent."

We are called to repent.

The Holy Spirit will pursue us, convict us and plead for us to repent and return to the Lord.

Joel 2:12-13 says,

> "'Yet even now,' declares the Lord, 'return to me with all your heart, with fasting, with weeping with mourning; and rend your hearts and not your garments.' Return to the Lord your God, for he is gracious and merciful, slow to anger, and abounding in steadfast love; and he relents over disaster."

Repentance is more than admitting we did something wrong. It's being grieved that we fell back into sin. When the Israelites sinned, they would cut up their clothes *(rend means to tear)* to show God how sorry they were for their actions. This passage is saying that our hearts should be all torn up inside due to our sin.

What's so beautiful is God wants us to return to Him because He is gracious and merciful, abounding in love for us, no matter how far we've fallen away.

Romans 2:4 says,

> "Or do you presume on the riches of his kindness and forbearance and patience, not knowing that God's kindness is meant to lead you to repentance?"

Knowing that God has open arms of forgiveness should cause us to run to Him with rendered, repentant hearts. Repentance doesn't just make us positionally right with God again. It leads us back into His presence where we can again have Him as our first love and focus in our lives.

Acts 3:19-20 says,

> "Repent therefore, and turn back, that your sins may be blotted out, that times of refreshing may come from the presence of the Lord, and that he may send the Christ appointed for you, Jesus."

We are refreshed in His presence, knowing that our hearts are right with Him again. Then, we can move forward in further transformation from the inside out.

> "If a man does not repent, God will whet his sword; he has bent and readied his bow." -Psalm 7:12
>
> "Bear fruit in keeping with repentance." -Matthew 3:8
>
> "Repent, therefore, of this wickedness of yours, and pray to the Lord that, if possible, the intent of your heart may be forgiven you." -Acts 8:22
>
> "Remember, then, what you received and heard. Keep it, and repent. If you will not wake up, I will come like a thief, and you will not know at what hour I will come against you." -Revelation 3:3
>
> "Yet if they turn their heart in the land to which they have been carried captive, and repent and plead with you in the land of the captors, saying, 'We have sinned and have acted perversely and wickedly.' If they repent with all their hart and with all their soul in the land of their enemies, who carried them captive, and pray to you toward their land, which you gave to their fathers, the city that you have chosen, and the house that I have built for your name, then hear in heaven your dwelling place their prayer and their plea, and maintain their cause and forgive your people who have sinned against you, and all their transgressions that they have committed against you, and grant them compassion in the sight of those who carried them captive, that they may have compassion on them." -1 Kings 8:47-50

"But David's heart struck him after he had numbered the people. And David said to the Lord, 'I have sinned greatly in what I have done. But now, O Lord, please take away the iniquity of your servant, for I have done very foolishly.'"
-2 Samuel 24:10

TAKE A MOMENT

1. What has repentance looked like for you in the past?

2. How might you want to engage in repentance differently moving forward?

> *Heavenly Father, thank You that the Holy Spirit will convict me when my heart leads me astray. Thank You that Your love and mercy openly waits for me to come to You with a rendered, repentant heart when I have wandered. May I be quick to repent and turn from my sin so that I can be refreshed in Your presence. Thank You that You rebuild, restore, and renew the places in my heart that continually need to be transformed. Amen.*

DAY 37
CLEAN HEART

Our homes are to be our safe retreat from the world. A place where we can be our true selves, putting on our comfy clothes to relax and rejuvenate. The reality is, our homes can be the busiest, most tension-filled environments we experience. Unless you live alone, you live with other sin-filled people who also need their hearts desperately cleaned by the Savior. Some may be followers of Jesus; some may not. If there are unbelievers in your home, they don't even have the Holy Spirit inside of them to help them overcome their flesh and temptations. It's even harder for them to live out anything that resembles the fruit of the Spirit: love, joy, peace, patience, kindness, goodness, faithfulness, gentleness, and self-control.

One of the most critical places to ponder how our hearts are doing is to observe how we respond and react to the people who live inside our home. Maybe you have a roommate that has different standards of cleanliness. Maybe your in-laws or parents live with you, and it gets confusing who is in control of the household. Perhaps you have a blended marriage with step-children, and it feels complicated to know how to lead and guide them. Maybe you are living with your adult children who have different lifestyle choices than you. We cannot control the hearts of those who live within the walls of our homes, but we can control ours. How are we choosing to love, forgive, give grace, resolve conflict, and not hold on to hurt or bitterness? Maybe this is where we need to pray for a clean heart next.

James 4:8 says,

> "Draw near to God, and he will draw near to you. Cleanse your hands, you sinners, and purity your hearts, you double-minded."

We cannot appear to have a clean heart when we engage with our neighbors, friends, and co-workers and then allow the sin in our hearts to creep out with our family and roommates in our homes. That is hypercritical and being double-minded. When we are tired and want a day off, we can truly see if we are living in our flesh or drawing near to God to cleanse our hearts.

A double life can occur when what we do at home is not what we do in public. Are you calm with everyone but your children and spouse? Do you give grace to those you lead but not those you live with? A double life can occur by what we do when we are alone. What do we look at on our phones or computers that is inappropriate? What do we do in our bedrooms that we want to keep behind locked doors? We need to continue to do surgery on our hearts if we're going to live in integrity.

Psalm 101:2 says,

> "I will ponder the way that is blameless. Oh when will you come to me? I will walk with integrity of heart within my house."

To have a clean heart, we must have integrity.

Who we are at home is who we are in our hearts. No one should be able to blame us for sinful attitudes or actions if we are pursuing holiness. This is the best witness we can have with non-believers who live with us. When they see our transformation at home, they will know our change is real. It may even increase their desire for transformation.

I Thessalonians 3:12-13 says,

> "May the Lord make you increase and abound in love for one another and for all, as we do for you, so that he may establish your hearts blameless in holiness before our God and Father, at the coming of our Lord Jesus with all his saints."

A clean heart is a blameless heart. Maybe this is the next place we need to invite our Holy God to clean so that we can transform from the inside out.

> "Cast away from you all the transgressions that you have committed, and make yourselves a new heart and a new spirit! Why will you die, O house of Israel?" -Ezekiel 18:31

> "And I will give you a new heart, and a new spirit I will put within you. And I will remove the heart of stone from your flesh and give you a heart of flesh." -Ezekiel 36:26

> "And God, who knows the heart, bore witness to them, by giving them the Holy Spirit just as he did to us, and he made no distinction between us and them, having cleansed their hearts by faith." -Acts 15:8-9

> "Let us draw near with a true heart in full assurance of faith, with our hearts sprinkled clean from an evil conscience and our bodies washed with pure water." -Hebrews 10:22

TAKE A MOMENT

1. In what ways can you further clean your heart when you are at home?

2. Why is living with integrity when no one is around important?

> *Heavenly Father, I know that having a clean heart at home is impossible without Your Spirit's empowerment. I pray as King David did in Psalm 51:10, "Create in me a clean heart, O God, and renew a right spirit within me." Give me love, patience, kindness, and self-control with those I live with. Help me to walk in integrity when I am alone. Help me pursue blamelessness to be an example to those I live with of how Your power changes people when we invite You to transform us. Amen.*

DAY 38
GOD'S LOVE IN MY HEART

Surgery is not always about just taking something out like a tumor or our intestines. Surgery may also be about putting something into us to help us experience life more fully. It may be a new kidney, heart or blood infusion. God's surgery on us requires both removing and inserting. He removes our sinful tendencies from our hearts when we invite Him to do so. He also infuses our hearts with His unconditional love so that we will continue to have our hearts tethered to His. When we know that He loves us and we can tangibly experience His love, our hearts long to be transformed to become just like Him. The more we become like Him, the more we will experience the fullness of God.

After traveling the world to 30 countries as a missionary, I have come to believe that the two greatest desires of people in any culture are: to be fully known *(all of our good and all of our bad)* as well as fully loved *(there are no conditions placed on receiving it)*. This love is impossible to experience outside of Christ. He is the only one who knows us better than we know ourselves. He is the one who knows the depravity in our hearts, and He was the one willing to die for it. He is the one who opens His arms, again and again, saying, "Come to Me. I love you. Experience My love. It will forever change you." Jesus forgives fully without looking back. He loves extravagantly without requiring it in return. He showers grace on us when we deserve judgment. The Beatles had it right when they wrote the lyrics, "All you need is love. Love! Love is all you need." Our greatest need is Jesus' love in our hearts.

We may know that Jesus loves us, for the Bible tells us so, but how can we experience His love deep in our hearts?

Ephesians 3:16-19 says,

> "That according to the riches of his glory he may grant you to be strengthened with power through his Spirit in your inner being, so that Christ may dwell in your hearts through faith- that you, being rooted and grounded in love, may have strength to comprehend with all the saints what is the breadth and length and height and depth, and to know the love of Christ that surpasses knowledge, that you may be filled up with all the fullness of God."

This extremely long sentence which is the Apostle Paul's prayer to the church in Ephesus, is packed with spiritual truth, that when understood, can change our hearts forever.

God wants us to be strengthened by His Spirit, who lives inside us, to understand the depth of Christ's love for us fully. The Spirit will help us experientially know Christ's love in a way beyond human understanding and human ability. We won't be able to articulate it. His love is all-consuming, ever-flowing, always present. We can't run from it. When Paul says we are to try to grasp how high, deep, and wide Christ's love is, He wants us to picture ourselves so securely placed in Christ that we will experience the fullness of God's unimaginable presence and fullness.

Though our hearts are deceitful, the Holy Spirit can bring us hope by pouring God's unconditional love into our hearts. We are forgiven. We are chosen. We have been given grace and mercy. He has a plan for our lives. When we experience God's love, our focus is solely on Him, and our sinful nature no longer consumes us. Christ's love transforms our hearts from the inside out. Let us rest in His love today.

"And hope does not put us to shame, because God's love has been poured into our hearts through the Holy Spirit who has been given to us." -Romans 5:5

"May the Lord direct your hearts to the love of God and to the steadfastness of Christ." -2 Thessalonians 3:5

"Who shall separate us from the love of Christ? Shall tribulation, or distress, or persecution, or famine, or nakedness, or danger, or sword? As it is written, "For your sake we are being killed all the day long; we are regarded as sheep to be slaughtered." No, in all these things we are more than conquerors through him who loved us. For I am sure that neither death nor life, nor angels nor rulers, nor things present nor things to come, nor powers, nor height nor depth, nor anything else in all creation, will be able to separate us from the love of God in Christ Jesus our Lord." -Romans 8:35-39

"For the love of Christ controls us, because we have concluded this: that one has died for all, therefore all have died; and he died for all, that those who live might no longer live for themselves but for him who for their sake died and was raised." -2 Corinthians 5:14

"But you, beloved, building yourselves up in your most holy faith and praying in the Holy Spirit, keep yourselves in the love of God, waiting for the mercy of our Lord Jesus Christ that leads to eternal life." -Jude 1: 20-21

TAKE A MOMENT

1. Meditate on how much Christ loves you. Sit in His presence for five more minutes *(set a timer even)* and invite the Holy Spirit to help you experience Christ's, all-consuming love. Allow it to flow over you and consume you.

2. Knowing His love is available for you at any moment and without restraint, how can you rest more often in His love to help your heart stay focused on Him?

> *Heavenly Father, thank You for Your Spirit that has been placed in my life to help me comprehend and experience the love of Christ. May Christ's love consume me in such a way that my desires completely change. I want to be so overwhelmed by His love that my focus is on Him and Him alone. Amen.*

DAY 39

GOD ENLARGES MY HEART

In Dr. Seuss's book, *"How the Grinch Stole Christmas,"* we see the Grinch is all about destroying everything having to do with Christmas. He is mean-spirited, ruthless, and a bully. He has no friends and no joy until he meets Cindy Lou. Cindy believes that the Grinch could be different. She believes that his heart, that is three sizes too small, can grow and care for others. She doesn't give up. She pursues him. She invites him to a Christmas event. And sure enough, the Grinch begins to change. His heart grows for the people of Whoville, and he restores what he destroyed and returns what he stole.

Though we may not immediately relate to being compassionless thieves in the night like the Grinch, we just may relate to him when it comes to having a heart three sizes too small. Our human hearts are too small on their own to live out what God asks us to be and do. To have a God-sized heart, we must ask Him to enlarge it.

Psalm 119:32 says,

> "I will run in the way of your commandments when you enlarge my heart!"

When we invite God to enlarge our hearts, we: care for the poor, love the unlovely, forgive the unforgivable, and have compassion for the lost. To live these character traits out, we must ask God to make our hearts as big as His is for those around us.

When God enlarges our hearts, we see the needs of those around us. We see their depravity and have compassion for them instead of hatred. This moves us to pray for their salvation and for God to direct their hearts toward Him, so that, they might be saved from their sin and destruction.

1 Chronicles 29:18 says,

> "O Lord, the God of Abraham, Isaac, and Israel, our fathers, keep forever such purposes and thoughts in the hearts of your people, and direct their hearts toward you."

God is the one who enlarges our hearts so that we would pray for others' salvation. It is not natural in our hearts to pray for others. It is when we ask God to give us His heart that we can do so.

> "That he may incline our hearts to him, to walk in all his ways and to keep his commandments, his statues, and his rules, which he commanded our fathers." -1 Kings 8:58

TAKE A MOMENT

1. What sort of people do you need to ask God to enlarge your heart for?

2. Who can you pray for that needs salvation?

> *Heavenly Father, please enlarge my heart to care for the people around me. Enable me to see the lost people around me to pray for them and to take the steps of faith to share Jesus with them. Enlarge my heart to care for the poor, to forgive those who have hurt me, and to love those who are difficult to love. Grow my heart to be like Yours. Amen.*

DAY 40

GOD'S SPIRIT IN MY HEART

This is our last devotional together, but the journey of transforming our hearts is just beginning. We are now convinced that our hearts are deceitful and depraved. We understand that we cannot change our hearts just by trying harder. We can only see heart transformation if we continually invite God to convict us and empower us. God has given us the gift of the Holy Spirit in our hearts to do this.

Galatians 4:6 says,

> "And because you are sons, God has sent the Spirit of his Son into our hearts, crying, 'Abba! Father!'"

The Holy Spirit lives inside us to transform the darkness in our hearts into the image of Christ. We cannot expect heart change without Him.

God has given us the Spirit to help us know what we should do and empower us to be able to do it.

John 14:26 says,

> "But the Helper, the Holy Spirit, whom the Father will send in my name, he will teach you all things and bring to your remembrance all that I have said to you."

God will remind us what we have learned and show us how to live it out.

When we invite the Spirit to empower us daily, we will see consistent growth in our lives. We will always have our sin-filled hearts with us until we are wholly sanctified in Heaven, but God has given us the Holy Spirit so that we can live victoriously over our flesh today.

Galatians 5:16-18 says,

> "But I say, walk by the Spirit, and you will not gratify the desires of the flesh. For the desires of the flesh are against the Spirit, and the desires of the Spirit are against the flesh, for these are opposed to each other, to keep you from doing the things you want to do. But if you are led by the Spirit, you are not under the law."

We may not fully know how to ask the Spirit to empower us toward change, and that's ok because the Spirit prays for us on our behalf.

Romans 8:26-27 says,

> "Likewise the Spirit helps us in our weakness. For we do not know what to pray for as we ought, but the Spirit himself intercedes for us with groanings too deep for words. And he who searches hearts knows what is the mind of the Spirit, because the Spirit intercedes for the saints according to the will of God."

We may not know what to pray so that our hearts become more like Christ, but the Spirit does. When we invite Him to help us in our weaknesses, He will be faithful to do so.

God's will for us is to be Spirit-filled, not sin-filled. If we don't grasp that God's will for us is to be empowered by the Spirit, we will live foolish, deceived, disempowered lives that have no hope of truly transforming from the inside out.

Ephesians 5:17-18 says,

> "Therefore, do not be foolish, but understand what the will of the Lord is. And do not get drunk with wine, for that is debauchery, but be filled with the Spirit."

Just as someone who is drunk needs to keep drinking to stay drunk, we continually invite the Spirit to empower us to remain empowered. His faithful empowerment enables us to have the heart of God toward anyone in any circumstances. His power helps us say "no" to our flesh and "yes" to pursuing holiness and right living.

Zachariah 4:6 says,

> "Not by might, nor by power, but by my Spirit, say the Lord of hosts."

We cannot change our hearts in our own wisdom and might. It is only through the Spirit's power that we can become like Christ. May we continue to have our hearts transformed from the inside out by inviting the Holy Spirit to give us wisdom to know what is right and the power to live it out. He will surely do it!

> "And do not grieve the Holy Spirit of God, by whom you were sealed for the day of redemption." -Ephesians 4:30

> "And who has also put his seal on us and given us his Spirit in our hearts as a guarantee." -2 Corinthians 1:22

> "If you then, who are evil, know how to give good gifts to your children, how much more will the heavenly Father give the Holy Spirit to those who ask him!" -Luke 11:13

> "For he whom God has sent utters the words of God, for he gives the Spirit without measure." -John 3:34

“When the Spirit of truth comes, he will guide you into all the truth, for he will not speak on his own authority, but whatever he hears he will speak, and he will declare to you the things that are to come.” -John 16:13

“For those who live according to the flesh set their minds on the things of the flesh, but those who live according to the Spirit set their minds on the things of the Spirit. For to set the mind on the flesh is death, but to set the mind on the Spirit is life and peace.” -Romans 8:5-6

“If the Spirit of him who raised Jesus from the dead dwells in you, he who raised Christ Jesus from the dead will also give life to your mortal bodies through his Spirit who dwells in you.” -Romans 8:11

TAKE A MOMENT

1. How can you intentionally invite the Spirit to empower you daily so that you stay on this journey of transformation?

2. How much have you grown in the past 40 days when it comes to knowing your heart and actively working at transforming it? Who else might want to grow from the inside out that you can come alongside and go through this devotional together?

> *Heavenly Father, I need the Holy Spirit to empower me so that I can continue to have my heart transformed to be more like Christ's. Thank You for not expecting me to change on my own but giving me Your power to live life in a way that is honoring You. Remind me daily to invite the Spirit to empower me to be in Your will when it comes to what I think, feel, and do. You are the great Surgeon. Thank You for operating on my heart and making me more like You. Amen*